P9-ARQ-284

The First Book of
VICE-PRESIDENTS
OF THE UNITED STATES
★—★—★

BY JOHN D. AND EMALIE P. FEERICK
Illustrated with Engravings and Photographs

Revised Edition

A First Book

FRANKLIN WATTS, INC.

New York/London

Updated 1981

To Maureen Grace

We acknowledge with deep appreciation the gracious assistance of Miss Linda Plaza, who typed and retyped the manuscript.

Photographs courtesy of the Library of Congress, except for the following: The White House: p. 89; Republican County Committee of New York: p. 90; United Press International: pp. 91 and 92.

Library of Congress Cataloging in Publication Data

Feerick, John D
The first book of vice-presidents of the United States.

  (A First book)
  Includes index.
  SUMMARY: An introduction to the office of Vice-President, with brief sketches of the men who have filled that post.
  1. Vice-Presidents — United States — Biography — Juvenile literature. [1. Vice-Presidents] I. Feerick, Emalie P., joint author. II. Title.
E176.8.F43 1977   973'.0992 [B]   77-1454
ISBN 0-531-02907-7

UPDATED 1981

Third Edition

Contents

The Office of Vice-President

Creation of the Office

FIFTY-FIVE delegates attended the Constitutional Convention of 1787, at which the Constitution of the United States was written. They spent most of their time discussing the office of President and the legislature. It was not until near the end of the convention that the office of Vice-President was even proposed.

On September 4, 1787, a committee composed of one delegate from each of the states present recommended that there be an office of Vice-President. It was proposed that the Vice-President be elected in the same manner as the President, that he be the immediate successor to the President, and that he also hold the office of president of the Senate.

In the discussion that followed, a number of delegates criticized the plan. But finally, the office of Vice-President was created by a vote of eight states to two. (Twelve states were represented at the Constitutional Convention, but when the vote was taken North Carolina abstained and New York was not represented.)

Election of the Vice-President

THE CONSTITUTION establishes a four-year term for the Vice-President. It also provides that he is to be elected at the same time and in the same manner as the President. Under the original method of election of President and Vice-President, Presidential electors were selected in each state to vote for two persons for President. The candidate who received the second-highest number of votes would become Vice-President. The framers of the Constitution wanted the Vice-President to be the second-best man for the Presidency. This

3

idea worked well during the first two Presidential elections, in which John Adams was the runner-up to George Washington. But in the third election, for the first and only time in American history, the Presidency and the Vice-Presidency became occupied by persons of different political parties. John Adams, a Federalist, was elected President. Thomas Jefferson, a Democratic-Republican, was elected Vice-President.

In the Presidential election of 1800 most of the Democratic-Republican electors voted for Thomas Jefferson and Aaron Burr, intending that Jefferson be President and Burr be Vice-President. Since Burr received as many votes as Jefferson, there was a tie. The House of Representatives, required to choose between the two, elected Jefferson President.

As a result of this election the Twelfth Amendment to the Constitution was adopted in 1804. The amendment requires the electors to cast two ballots — one for President and the other for Vice-President. The Twelfth Amendment also provides that the qualifications for Vice-President be the same as for President. Thus the Vice-President must be a natural-born citizen of the United States, must be at least thirty-five years of age, and must have been a resident within the United States for at least fourteen years.

In addition, the Twelfth Amendment provides that the candidate having the greatest number of votes for Vice-President, if it is a majority, becomes Vice-President. If no candidate receives a majority, the Senate chooses as Vice-President one of the candidates having the two highest numbers of votes. The only time that this provision has been used was when Richard M. Johnson received exactly one-half of the electoral votes in 1836. Since this was one vote less than a majority, the Senate had to choose a Vice-President. Johnson was chosen.

The nomination of a person for either President or Vice-President is not provided for by the Constitution. It is customary for the political parties to hold nominating conventions during every Presidential election year. Each party nominates a person for President

4

and a person for Vice-President. In order to attract the highest number of votes for its candidates, each nominating convention often selects a Presidential candidate from one section of the country and a Vice-Presidential candidate from another. Many times candidates from different factions of a party are placed together on a ticket in order to unite the party.

Usually the Presidential candidate has much to say about the selection of his running mate. Because the relationship between the Vice-President and the President is so important, it is good for the Presidential candidate to have this influence.

The people vote on the Tuesday after the first Monday in November of every year divisible by four. What really happens is that the people vote for electors from their state. The Constitution entitles each state to one elector for each of its members of Congress. (In addition, under the Twenty-third Amendment, the District of Columbia has three electoral votes.) The party that receives the most popular votes in a state receives all the electoral votes for that state. In December there are state meetings of the electors of the party that received the most votes in November. They vote for the Presidential and Vice-Presidential candidates of their party. On the sixth day of the following January, the president of the Senate opens the certificates of the electors and the votes are counted. To be elected either President or Vice-President a candidate must have a majority of the electoral votes. (On several occasions in American history the candidate with a majority of the electoral votes had fewer popular votes than his major opponent.) The winning candidates take office on January 20.

Inauguration of the Vice-President

BEFORE THE ADOPTION of the Twentieth Amendment in 1933, the terms of the President and Vice-President did not begin until March 4. The Twentieth Amendment provides that the terms of President and Vice-President end at noon on January 20. At some point after noon the new President and Vice-President take their oaths of office.

The Constitution contains no oath of office for the Vice-President as it does for the President. It was therefore necessary for a law to be passed establishing an oath of office for the Vice-President. The present oath, which is the same as that taken by other government officials, is:

"I, A. B. (name), do solemnly swear (or affirm) that I will support and defend the Constitution of the United States against all enemies, foreign and domestic; that I will bear true faith and allegiance to the same; that I take this obligation freely, without any mental reservation or purpose of evasion; and that I will well and faithfully discharge the duties of the office on which I am about to enter. So help me God."

The Presidential oath usually has been administered to the President by the Chief Justice of the United States. But various officials have administered the oath to the Vice-President. Until 1860, the president pro tempore (temporary president) of the Senate normally performed this function. Then, the outgoing Vice-President administered it. If he had died, resigned, succeeded to the Presidency, or been elected to a second term, the president pro tempore administered it instead. In the past thirty years the oath has been administered to the Vice-President by outgoing Vice-Presidents, Senate party leaders, a Supreme Court Justice, and speakers of the House of Representatives.

Before 1937, the Vice-President usually took his oath in the Senate chamber. Following this ceremony, the newly elected President would be sworn in on the portico (balcony) in front of the Capitol. Since 1937, when the changes enacted by the Twentieth Amendment were followed for the first time, both the President and Vice-President have been sworn in on the portico of the Capitol — the President first.

Compensation of the Vice-President

THE CONSTITUTION states that the President shall receive a compensation for his services. There is no similar provision for the Vice-President.

The question of whether the Vice-President should receive a salary arose during the First Congress. Some members of the House of Representatives felt that he should be paid on a daily basis because he would have so little work to do. James Madison believed that it would be offensive to the dignity of the second officer of the government if the Vice-President were not given an annual salary. An annual salary of $5,000 was finally agreed upon.

Today the Vice-President receives:

An annual salary of	$79,125
An annual expense allowance of	$10,000

He is also provided with:

A staff of over 40 people
Secret Service agents for protection
Offices in the Capitol, the Senate office building,
    and the executive office building
His own seal and flag

From time to time there has been talk of giving the Vice-President an official residence. Early in 1966, Congress finally authorized an appropriation for a Vice-Presidential mansion to be constructed on the Naval Observatory grounds in Washington, D.C. However, construction was postponed.

Duties of the Vice-President

PRESIDENT OF THE SENATE

THE CONSTITUTION gives the Vice-President the duty of presiding over the Senate. In this capacity he has the power to cast tie-breaking votes and to open the certificates of the Presidential electors designating their votes for President and Vice-President.

In the early days of the nation the Vice-President had a great deal of influence in the Senate because of his position as president of that body. He appointed members of the Senate to committees, made rulings, and decided disputes concerning the certificates of the Presidential electors. The first Vice-President, John Adams, took an active part in Senate debates. Adams used his tie-breaking vote twenty-nine times, more than any other Vice-President. As time went on, this authority of the Vice-President as president of the Senate diminished. Today the Vice-President seldom presides over the Senate. When the Vice-President is absent from the Senate, the president pro tempore presides. When neither of them is present, another senator, appointed by the president pro tempore, presides over the Senate. Often, this duty falls to a junior senator, providing him with good training in parliamentary procedure.

IMMEDIATE SUCCESSOR TO PRESIDENT

THE SECOND major duty that the Constitution gives the Vice-President is to discharge the powers and duties of President in case of the death, resignation, removal, or inability of the President. It is strange that the chief role the Vice-President has played in history — succession to the Presidency — received little attention at the Constitutional Convention.

On April 4, 1841, President William Henry Harrison died in office, only one month after his inauguration. Vice-President John

Tyler asserted his right to the office and became President for the remainder of the term. Seven other Vice-Presidents have since exercised their right to the Presidency upon the death of a President. Those who did so were: Vice-President Millard Fillmore, when President Zachary Taylor died on July 9, 1850; Andrew Johnson, when Abraham Lincoln died by assassination on April 15, 1865; Chester A. Arthur, when James A. Garfield died on September 19, 1881, of wounds caused by an assassin's bullet; Theodore Roosevelt, when William McKinley died September 14, 1901, eight days after he was shot by an assassin; Calvin Coolidge, when Warren Harding died on August 2, 1923; Harry S Truman, when Franklin D. Roosevelt died on April 12, 1945; and Lyndon B. Johnson, when John F. Kennedy was assassinated on November 22, 1963.

On no occasion in American history has a Vice-President acted as President when a President became disabled in office. This has been partly because of uncertainty as to whether the Constitution permits the Vice-President to act as President for a temporary period of time. It is also because the Constitution did not specifically authorize anyone to declare the President disabled. Following President Kennedy's assassination, these defects in the Constitution received much public attention. As a result, on July 6, 1965, Congress proposed the Twenty-fifth Amendment to the Constitution. Under this amendment the Vice-President and the Cabinet are given the power to declare the President disabled, and in case of inability the Vice-President is authorized to act as President until the President recovers. The amendment also empowers the President to nominate a person for Vice-President whenever that office becomes vacant. Congress then would have to vote upon the nomination. If a majority of each house approved, the nominee would become Vice-President.

OTHER DUTIES

UNTIL the twentieth century the Vice-President had few responsibilities other than to preside over the Senate and to be the immediate successor to the President. It was therefore not unusual in the nineteenth century for Vice-Presidents to spend little time in the nation's capital. They often lived somewhere else and kept busy doing work unrelated to the office of Vice-President.

In recent years there has been a remarkable change in the office of Vice-President. It has become a vital part of the governmental machinery. Today, it is customary for the Vice-President to sit as a regular member of the President's Cabinet, and to preside there if the President is absent. The Vice-President is a member of the National Security Council, attends conferences held between the President and the leaders of Congress and between the President and his key foreign-policy advisers, represents the President at home and abroad, and consults with the President on various political matters. He is chairman of the National Aeronautics Space Council and of the Advisory Council of the Peace Corps. He is also the coordinator of various governmental programs. Because of his position as president of the Senate, the Vice-President is able to help get the President's programs through Congress.

Recent Vice-Presidents have been especially active in Presidential missions and goodwill tours throughout the world. These missions have brought the Vice-Presidents into contact with world leaders and have made them personally familiar with world problems. Moreover, the Vice-Presidents have acted and negotiated on behalf of the United States, and have returned to this country with detailed reports of their findings and activities.

The Vice-President has truly become a fully informed, consulted, and working member of the government. The office of Vice-President has achieved a new dimension.

The Vice-Presidents

John Adams

JOHN ADAMS, the first Vice-President of the United States and the second President, was born October 30, 1735, on his father's farm in Braintree (now Quincy), Massachusetts. He worked on this farm as a young boy. Although at first he was not very studious, he began to take his studies seriously when he realized he would not be accepted by the college of his choice. At the age of sixteen Adams entered Harvard, where he was an excellent speaker and one of the best scholars in the class. After his graduation from Harvard in 1755, he began teaching Latin in Worcester, Massachusetts, while at the same time studying law. In 1758 he was admitted to the Boston bar. He then opened a law office in Braintree and started to build a prosperous law practice.

In 1764 Adams married Abigail Smith, the daughter of a minister. She was an intelligent woman with whom he could discuss almost any problem. They had three sons and two daughters. The first son, John Quincy Adams, became the sixth President of the United States, the only son of a President to become President.

Adams became a leader of the colonial movement for independence. When the British Parliament passed the Stamp Act in an attempt to impose a direct tax on the American colonists, even though the colonists had no representation in Parliament, Adams led the opposition to the act. He demonstrated his courage after the Boston Massacre when he defended one of the British officers and several of his men in court. In 1774 and 1775, Adams served as a delegate to the First and Second Continental Congresses. He fought for and helped with the writing of the Declaration of Independence. He was also one of the signers of that great charter of liberty.

In 1776 Adams became the first head of the War Department, and in 1778, at the age of forty-three, he was sent as an ambassador to France, where he succeeded in getting loans for the colonies. In 1780 he went to Holland (now The Netherlands) and again succeeded in obtaining money needed to continue the American Revolution. In 1782 Adams negotiated the treaty of peace with Great Britain, and in 1785 he became our first minister to Great Britain under the Articles of Confederation. He was still in England when the Constitution was written and therefore was not among its signers.

In the first election held under the Constitution, George Washington received the highest number of electoral votes and became President. Since Adams received the second-highest number of votes, he became Vice-President.

Adams proved to be an effective Vice-President. As president of the Senate he was a strong supporter of various programs of the administration. Washington respected Adams and consulted with him frequently. In 1792 Washington was unanimously reelected President, and Adams was reelected Vice-President. In 1796, after Washington had declined to run for another term, Adams was elected President. He thus became the first of only seven Vice-Presidents who were later elected President. Thomas Jefferson, the leader of the opposition, was elected Vice-President. As President, Adams' main achievement was keeping the United States neutral during the French Revolution and the wars in Europe that followed it. He was the first President to live in the White House.

In 1800, Adams sought reelection but was defeated by Vice-President Jefferson. He then retired to his Massachusetts farm, where he spent much of his time reading and writing. On March 4, 1825, he saw his son inaugurated President. He died at the age of ninety on July 4, 1826, exactly fifty years after the signing of the Declaration of Independence. His dying words were: "Thomas Jefferson still survives." Adams did not know that Jefferson had died earlier that same day. Adams is buried in Boston.

Thomas Jefferson

THOMAS JEFFERSON, the second Vice-President and the third President, was born April 13, 1743, on one of his father's tobacco plantations in Goochland County (now Albemarle County), Virginia. He was the third of ten children. When his father died, Jefferson, the oldest son, became the head of the family, inheriting his father's land. He was then only fourteen years old. Jefferson studied Greek and Latin at a private school, and at the age of sixteen, he entered the College of William and Mary. Especially fond of music, mathematics, and architecture, he compiled a brilliant record as a student. After graduating from college in 1762, he studied law under George Wythe, a noted lawyer and judge. At the age of twenty-four, Jefferson was admitted to the Virginia bar.

In 1769, after having served for a brief period as a justice of the peace, Jefferson became a member of the Virginia legislature. He served there for five years, working with Patrick Henry and others for colonial independence. During this period, on January 1, 1772, he married Martha Wayles Skelton, a beautiful young widow. She died before their eleventh wedding anniversary. They had five daughters and one son, but only two daughters lived beyond infancy.

In 1775 Jefferson was named a delegate to the Second Continental Congress. The following year he, John Adams, Benjamin Franklin, Robert R. Livingston, and Roger Sherman drafted the

Declaration of Independence. Jefferson was actually the one who wrote this historic document. During the next ten years Jefferson served as a member of the Virginia legislature, as governor of Virginia, and as a member of Congress under the Articles of Confederation. Along with Benjamin Franklin and John Adams, he was sent to France to negotiate commercial treaties in Europe. While serving in the Virginia legislature, he sponsored several measures to reform Virginia law. One of his major achievements there was the Virginia Charter of Religious Freedom.

In 1785 the Continental Congress elected him to succeed Franklin as minister to France, and in 1789 George Washington made him our first Secretary of State. Jefferson often disagreed with Alexander Hamilton, Washington's Secretary of the Treasury. Jefferson believed in the ability of the common people to govern themselves. Hamilton favored an aristocratic government. Their differences resulted in the formation of the first political parties. Hamilton's followers were called Federalists, and Jefferson's were called Democratic-Republicans.

In the election of 1796, Jefferson received the second-highest number of votes for President. He thus became Adams' Vice-President. The relationship between President and Vice-President during this term was not close because the two men were members of opposing parties. Nevertheless, election to the Vice-Presidency led to the Presidency for Jefferson just as it had for Adams. In 1800, Jefferson was elected President, and he served for two terms. He was the first President to be inaugurated in Washington, D.C. One of his greatest accomplishments was the purchase of the Louisiana Territory.

On March 4, 1809, when James Madison was inaugurated President, Jefferson retired to his Virginia estate, Monticello, which he had designed and built years before. During the remaining seventeen years of his life, he pursued his many and varied interests. He corresponded with Adams, invented various devices for his home, and founded the University of Virginia, designing the buildings himself. He died at Monticello on July 4, 1826, and is buried there.

Aaron Burr

THE THIRD Vice-President of the United States, Aaron Burr, was born on February 6, 1756, in Newark, New Jersey. His father was a Presbyterian minister and President of the College of New Jersey (now Princeton University). His mother was the daughter of a well-known Puritan minister named Jonathan Edwards. Both his parents died before Burr reached the age of three. He and his sister Sarah were raised by an uncle. They were tutored by a famous teacher named Tapping Reeve, whom Sarah later married.

Burr was a mischievous but bright child. At the age of thirteen he entered the College of New Jersey. He graduated three years later with honors. In 1774 he began to study theology. He soon discovered, however, that the religious life was not for him, and he took up the study of law in Connecticut.

At the outbreak of the American Revolution, Burr enlisted in the army. During the war he served under Benedict Arnold and later joined General George Washington's staff. He proved to be a brave soldier and was rapidly promoted — first to captain, then to major, and finally to lieutenant colonel. In 1779, after four years of military service, he resigned from the army because of poor health.

Burr resumed his study of law, and in 1782, at the age of twenty-six, began to practice in Albany, New York. That same year he married Theodosia Prevost, the widow of a British officer. She was ten years older than Burr. They had one daughter.

16

Toward the end of the war, Burr moved to New York City where he built up a reputation as a good lawyer and became active in state politics. He was elected to the state legislature in 1784, and in 1789 was appointed attorney general of New York by Governor George Clinton. In 1791, Burr was elected to the United States Senate, defeating Alexander Hamilton's father-in-law, General Philip Schuyler. He served only one term, during which he was noted for his great influence and overall ability. In 1794, Burr's wife died.

Burr's increasingly active role in the Democratic-Republican party between 1797 and 1799 led to his election as Vice-President under Thomas Jefferson in 1800.

As Vice-President, Burr excelled in his role as presiding officer of the Senate. In February, 1804, while still Vice-President, he became a candidate for governor of New York. The vigorous and often bitter opposition of Alexander Hamilton resulted in his defeat. No longer able to endure Hamilton's attacks on him, Burr challenged Hamilton to a duel at Weehawken, New Jersey. Hamilton was killed.

Burr's popularity took a sharp decline and he was not renominated for Vice-President. Following his retirement from the Vice-Presidency, Burr allegedly pursued a scheme to form, and then head, a separate republic in the southwestern United States. In 1807, before Chief Justice John Marshall, he was tried for treason and acquitted. But in 1808, after almost a year of persecution, he went to Europe to live. He remained there, living in poverty, until May of 1812, when he returned to the United States so that he could once again see his daughter. Unfortunately, their reunion never took place. That December, the ship on which she was traveling from South Carolina to New York was lost at sea.

It is reported that Burr returned to New York with less than ten dollars in his pocket. He went back to the practice of law, and due largely to his remarkable ability, he became one of the recognized leaders of his profession. He married again in 1833, but the marriage was an unhappy one that lasted only until 1834. On September 14, 1836, at the age of eighty, he died on Staten Island, New York. He is buried in Princeton, New Jersey.

George Clinton

GEORGE CLINTON, the fourth Vice-President of the United States, was the second to be elected to the office twice and the first to serve under two different Presidents.

Born on July 26, 1739, in Little Britain, New York, Clinton was the son of an Irish immigrant. He was educated by his father and a clergyman friend of the family. At the age of eighteen Clinton left home to become a sailor, but it was not long before he returned. During the French and Indian War he served as a lieutenant in the company led by his brother, General James Clinton.

When the war was over, Clinton studied law under Justice William Smith. He was admitted to the bar and made his home in Ulster, New York. By working hard he gained a reputation as a good lawyer. In particular, he became well known as a defender of freedom of speech and of the press.

In 1768, at twenty-nine years of age, Clinton became a member of the New York legislature. He served there until 1775, when he was elected to the Second Continental Congress. On February 7, 1770, Clinton married Cornelia Tappan, a member of a politically influential family in Ulster County. In December, 1775, the New York Provincial Congress commissioned him a brigadier general of the militia. The following year General George Washington ordered him to return to New York from the Continental Congress in order to help defend New York from the British. As a result, Clinton was not in Philadelphia for the signing of the Declaration of Independence, although he fully supported it.

In 1777, Clinton was made a brigadier general in the Continental Army and was elected first governor of New York. He was elected lieutenant governor in the same election, but he had to resign this post. He served as governor for seven three-year terms between 1777 and 1804. During this period he attended the Constitutional Convention of 1787, where he opposed the Constitution because he thought it made the federal government too powerful. Despite his opposition to the Constitution, Clinton was generally regarded as a man of great character and leadership, firmly pledged to democratic principles.

In 1804 he was chosen as Jefferson's Vice-President. In 1808, when it became clear that Jefferson would not run again, Clinton hoped to become the Democratic-Republican candidate for President. He thought he deserved the nomination, since two of the three previous Vice-Presidents had received it. He had to settle for the Vice-Presidential nomination, and was reelected, this time as James Madison's Vice-President.

During his second term Clinton suffered from poor health. In March, 1812, he became ill, and on April 20, 1812, he died of pneumonia in Washington, at the age of seventy-two. He was the first Vice-President to die in office. Clinton was buried in the Congressional Cemetery in Washington, but in 1907 his body was moved to Kingston, New York.

Elbridge Gerry

ELBRIDGE GERRY, the fifth Vice-President of the United States, was born on July 17, 1744, in Marblehead, Massachusetts. He was the third of twelve children born to a wealthy merchant. Gerry graduated from Harvard College at the age of eighteen and entered his father's business, which involved the shipping of dried codfish to foreign ports. In 1772 he was elected to the Massachusetts colonial legislature. From 1776 to 1781 he served as a delegate to the Second Continental Congress, and was a signer of the Declaration of Independence. Between 1783 and 1785 he served in Congress under the Articles of Confederation.

On January 12, 1786, Gerry married Ann Thompson, the daughter of a New York merchant. They had three sons and four daughters. Shortly after his marriage he returned to the Massachusetts legislature. The following year (1787) he was chosen to represent Massachusetts at the Constitutional Convention. Although he opposed the adoption of the Constitution, he became a loyal supporter of it once it had been ratified (approved) by his state. One of his main criticisms of the Constitution was that it did not contain a bill of rights. A bill of rights was added to the Constitution shortly after its adoption.

Gerry served in the House of Representatives in the First and Second Congresses of the United States. He then retired to his farm and devoted a good part of the next few years to his family. In 1797 President John Adams sent him to France with John Marshall and Charles C. Pinckney to negotiate a commercial treaty.

Beginning in 1800, Gerry ran for governor of Massachusetts four consecutive times, and was defeated each time. Finally, in 1810, he was elected governor and was reelected in 1811. During his second term Gerry signed a bill that reshaped election districts for state senators in order to give his party control of most of the districts. Upon seeing a map of the Democratic-Republican districts, one man thought it looked like a salamander. Someone else suggested that it should be called a "Gerrymander." Since that time the rearranging of election districts to the political advantage of one party has been called gerrymandering.

Gerry failed to be reelected governor in 1812. The Democratic-Republican party, however, nominated him for Vice-President. On the same ticket was President James Madison, who was seeking reelection. Although Gerry was then over sixty-eight years of age, he accepted the nomination and was elected.

He took the Vice-Presidential oath of office on March 4, 1813, at his home in Cambridge. Despite his age, Gerry enjoyed serving as Vice-President. His relationship with Madison was excellent and he frequently visited and consulted with the President.

On November 23, 1814, while on his way to the Senate, Gerry suddenly died. He was buried in the Congressional Cemetery in Washington, D.C., the only Vice-President buried in Washington today. His wife, who lived until 1849, was the last surviving widow of a signer of the Declaration of Independence.

Daniel D. Tompkins

THE SIXTH Vice-President of the United States, Daniel D. Tompkins, was born on June 21, 1774, in Fox Meadows (now Scarsdale), New York. His father was a Revolutionary patriot. Tompkins adopted the initial "D" while in school, so as to distinguish himself from a schoolmate who had the same name. In 1795, at the age of twenty-one, he graduated from Columbia College. Two years later he began practicing law in New York City. That same year he married Hannah Minthorne, the daughter of a prominent New York City Republican. They had seven children.

In 1801, Tompkins served as a member of the New York State constitutional convention, which revised the state constitution. In 1803 he was chosen a member of the New York legislature. The following year he was elected to the United States House of Representatives. He resigned before actually taking office to accept an appointment as an associate justice of the New York State Supreme Court, on which he served until 1807.

In that year Tompkins ran for the governorship of New York, and won. He held that office continuously for almost ten years. As governor, he became the most prominent political rival in New York of DeWitt Clinton, who had helped him to win the governorship in the first place.

One of Tompkins' most significant accomplishments occurred when, as governor of New York, he advocated the abolition of slavery in the state. As a result of his urging, the legislature set July 4, 1827, as the date when the abolition of slavery in New York would become effective.

During the War of 1812, Tompkins borrowed large amounts of money in his own name to help carry on the war. He was later accused of cheating the state when he could not produce accurate records of how the money had been spent. It later came to light that the state owed him thousands of dollars.

In 1814, Tompkins declined President Madison's offer to make him Secretary of State. In 1816, when he was reelected governor of New York, he was also elected Vice-President of the United States on the Democratic-Republican ticket with James Monroe. Restless as Vice-President, Tompkins ran for governor of New York in 1820 but was defeated by DeWitt Clinton. He was reelected to the Vice-Presidency in that year, however, when Monroe was reelected to the Presidency. During his second term as Vice-President, Tompkins suffered from poor health and spent little time in Washington. On June 11, 1825, three months after his term ended, he died on Staten Island, New York. He was just under fifty-one years of age. He is buried in St. Mark's Churchyard in New York City.

John Caldwell Calhoun

JOHN C. CALHOUN, the seventh Vice-President of the United States and the fourth to be elected for two terms, was the only one to resign from office. He was the first Vice-President not born a British subject, since he was born after the signing of the Declaration of Independence.

Calhoun was born on March 18, 1782, in Abbeville District, South Carolina. His father was an Irish immigrant farmer who was active in politics. Raised on a farm, Calhoun received little formal education but taught himself a great deal by reading. At the age of thirteen Calhoun entered a "log college" (classes held in a log cabin) run by his brother-in-law, Reverend Moses Waddel, who later became president of the University of Georgia. He studied there for a while, but when the school was temporarily closed in 1796, Calhoun returned to his farm. Calhoun continued to work there until the turn of the century. At the urging of an older brother, he returned to Waddel's college, which had been reopened. Then he attended Yale University. He graduated from Yale with honors in 1804, and went on to study law. In 1807, Calhoun opened an office in Abbeville District, and before long had a thriving practice. Calhoun's real interest, however, was politics.

His political career began in 1807, with a speech criticizing the British for interfering with American ships on the high seas. In 1808, at twenty-six years of age, he became a member of the South Carolina legislature, where he served until 1809. In 1811 he married Floride Bouneau of Charleston. They had nine children. In the same year that he was married he began his first term in the United States House of Representatives. He served there for three terms, becoming one of its most influential members. He was known as a "war hawk" because he was in favor of war with Britain. He also was regarded as one of the finest speakers in Congress. Said one person, "His gestures are easy and graceful, his language forcible . . . but above all, he confines himself closely to the subject, which he always understands and enlightens everyone within hearing, having said all a statesman should say, he is done."

In December, 1817, President James Monroe appointed Calhoun Secretary of War, a position in which he served with ability during Monroe's two terms. In 1824 he was elected Vice-President, and John Quincy Adams was elected President on the Democratic-Republican ticket. Four years later Calhoun became the Vice-Presidential running mate of Andrew Jackson, and they won. In 1832, while he was still Vice-President, the South Carolina legislature selected him to fill a vacant seat in the Senate. On December 28, 1832, he addressed the following letter to Secretary of State Edward Livingston: "Having concluded to accept of a seat in the United States Senate, I herewith resign the office of Vice-President of the United States."

Taking his seat in the Senate in 1833, he kept it for fifteen years, except for a short period when he served as Secretary of State under President John Tyler. Calhoun firmly believed in state sovereignty and thought that states had the right to secede (withdraw) from the Union. He also believed, however, that if they did secede and the Union were dissolved, it would be a disaster.

Calhoun died on March 31, 1850, in Washington, D. C., at the age of sixty-eight. He is buried in Charleston, South Carolina.

Martin Van Buren

MARTIN VAN BUREN was the eighth Vice-President of the United States and the third to be elected President.

Born on December 5, 1782, in Kinderhook, New York, Van Buren was the third of five children. His father, who was of Dutch descent and a veteran of the Revolutionary War, ran a tavern in Kinderhook. As a boy, Van Buren worked in the tavern. He listened carefully to the talk of the customers, some of whom were members of the New York legislature traveling to Albany. He received his formal education at the Kinderhook schoolhouse and the Kinderhook Academy. In 1796, at the age of fourteen, he began to study law. After finishing his training in a New York City law office, he was admitted to the bar in 1803, and then began to practice law in Kinderhook. In 1807 he married his childhood sweetheart, Hannah Hoes. They had four sons. His wife died in 1819.

In the year he married, Van Buren became counselor of the New York Supreme Court. In 1808, Governor Daniel Tompkins appointed him surrogate of Columbia County. Four years later he was elected to the New York State Senate as a Democratic-Republican, and in 1816 he was appointed attorney general of New York. Because of his political ability and warm personality, Van Buren became one of the leaders of the Democratic-Republican party in New York State.

In 1820 he was elected to the United States Senate, and in 1826 he was reelected. He resigned from the Senate when he was elected governor of New York in 1828, and then resigned as governor after serving only two months, to become President Andrew Jackson's Secretary of State. He was liked and trusted by Jackson. Before long he was the most influential member of the Cabinet. In 1831 he resigned as Secretary of State, and Jackson then appointed him minister to Great Britain. Confirmation of his appointment was denied by the Senate on January 25, 1832. Vice-President John Calhoun's tie-breaking vote was decisive in denying the appointment.

In May, 1832, Van Buren was nominated for Vice-President by the first convention of the newly formed Democratic party. Prior to 1832, Presidential and Vice-Presidential candidates were generally nominated by a congressional caucus. The caucus consisted of the members of the political party in Congress. The ticket chosen at the Democratic convention of 1832 was headed by President Jackson. Van Buren and Jackson were elected by a large majority.

As Vice-President, Van Buren was an able and fair presiding officer of the Senate. Always on close terms with President Jackson, he used his position as president of the Senate to promote the programs of the administration. In 1836, with Jackson's support, he was nominated for the Presidency by the Democratic convention, and in the election he received a clear majority of the votes. He was the first President born in New York, and the first born after the Declaration of Independence was signed. Soon after he took office, the country was plunged into its first great depression, the Panic of 1837. Because of it, Van Buren established the Independent Treasury, a government agency set up to handle public funds.

After being defeated for reelection in 1840, he retired to Lindenwald, his estate in Kinderhook. In 1848 he was an unsuccessful candidate for President on the Free Soil ticket. He died at Lindenwald on July 24, 1862, at the age of seventy-nine. He is buried in the Kinderhook Cemetery, Kinderhook, New York.

Richard Mentor Johnson

RICHARD M. JOHNSON, the ninth Vice-President of the United States and the first one to be elected by the Senate until Gerald R. Ford was chosen in 1973, was born on October 17, 1780, in a frontier settlement near Louisville, Kentucky. His father, who had migrated from Virginia to the West, was one of the early settlers of Kentucky.

Raised on the frontier, Johnson received few educational opportunities. At fifteen, however, he began to study Latin. He then took up the study of law under George Nicholas and James Brown at Transylvania University. He was admitted to the bar in 1802. Soon he was known as a good lawyer. He was elected to the Kentucky legislature in 1804, and in 1806 was elected to the United States House of Representatives. During the War of 1812, Johnson left Washington, although he kept his seat in Congress. He organized and became the colonel of a regiment of mounted Kentucky riflemen, and served under General William Henry Harrison. He fought gallantly, and was seriously wounded. He supposedly killed Tecumseh, the chief of the Shawnee Indians.

Johnson returned to Congress a war hero, and he served there until 1819, when he voluntarily retired. He was again elected a member of the Kentucky legislature, which promptly chose him to represent his state in the United States Senate. He served in the Senate until 1829, when he returned to the House of Representatives for another eight years. While in Congress, Johnson was a strong supporter of educational measures.

In 1836 he was nominated for the Vice-Presidency at the second Democratic national convention on a ticket headed by Martin Van Buren. During the campaign his supporters used the slogan, "Rumpsey, Dumpsey, Colonel Johnson killed Tecumseh." In the election, although Van Buren was elected President by a majority of the votes, Johnson received less than a majority for Vice-President. According to the Twelfth Amendment, the Senate then had to choose the Vice-President from the candidates having the two highest numbers of votes. Johnson was chosen over Francis Granger.

After leaving the Vice-Presidency in 1841, Johnson retired to Kentucky. In 1850 he returned to his state legislature. He died in Frankfort, Kentucky, on November 19, 1850 — eleven days after he had taken his seat in the legislature. He is buried in the State Cemetery in Frankfort.

John Tyler

JOHN TYLER was the first Vice-President to succeed to the Presidency upon the President's death in office. He established the precedent of a Vice-President becoming President for the remainder of a term when a President dies in office.

Tyler was born on March 29, 1790, in Charles City County, Virginia. He was the second son of John Tyler, a judge and a governor of Virginia, who was a close friend of Thomas Jefferson and Patrick Henry. Tyler attended school in Charles City, Virginia. In daring to oppose an unpopular schoolmaster, he displayed the independence that was to characterize his political life. After graduating from the College of William and Mary in 1807, he studied law under his father and was admitted to the bar in 1809. Two years later he was elected to the Virginia legislature, where he served five terms. On March 29, 1813, at the age of twenty-three, he married Letitia Christian. They had three sons and five daughters.

Tyler was elected to the United States House of Representatives in 1816, and served there until 1821, when he unsuccessfully ran for the Senate. He then was reelected to the Virginia legislature. In 1825 he became governor of Virginia. In 1827 he was elected to the United States Senate and was reelected in 1833. While serving in the Senate, Tyler strongly supported states' rights. He spoke his own mind on the issues of the day. In 1836, when the Virginia legislature tried to tell him how he should vote, he resigned from the Senate. Because of differences with President Jackson and other members of the Democratic party, he left the party and joined a new party known as the Whigs. In 1840 the Whigs unanimously nominated him for the Vice-Presidency on a ticket headed by General William Henry Harrison, a war hero. Harrison and Tyler, using the campaign slogan, "Tippecanoe and Tyler too," easily won the election.

On April 4, 1841, one month after becoming President, Harrison died in office. At the time, Tyler was at home in Williamsburg, Virginia. Upon being informed of the President's death, he immediately left for Washington, traveling by horseback and boat. When he arrived in Washington, there was some question as to whether he was the new President or was still Vice-President. Tyler maintained that he was now President. He took the Presidential oath, and assumed all the powers and duties of President.

As President, Tyler reorganized the Navy, established the Weather Bureau, opened the Orient to American trade, brought the Seminole War to an end, and approved statehood for Florida and Texas. His independent policies caused the Whigs to expel him from the party in September, 1841. Thus Tyler belonged to no political party for the rest of his term. During his term as President, his wife died. A little less than two years after his first wife's death, Tyler married Julia Gardiner of New York, becoming the first President to marry while in office. Tyler and his second wife had five sons and two daughters.

Upon leaving the Presidency in 1845, Tyler retired to his estate in Virginia and resumed the practice of law. He continued to take an active part in public affairs. When the Civil War broke out in 1861, Tyler tried to prevent secession. He later gave up hope of establishing peace and supported his state's secession from the Union. Tyler was elected to the Confederate (Southern) House of Representatives in November, 1861, but died in Richmond, Virginia, on January 18, 1862, before the legislative body met. His death was totally ignored by the government. However, in 1911, Congress authorized the erection of a monument to his memory in Hollywood Cemetery, Richmond, Virginia.

George Mifflin Dallas

GEORGE M. DALLAS, the eleventh Vice-President of the United States, was born on July 10, 1792, in Philadelphia, Pennsylvania. His father, Alexander James Dallas, was a lawyer and writer who later became President Madison's Secretary of the Treasury. Dallas attended the College of New Jersey, from which he graduated in 1810. Following his graduation, he studied law in his father's office and was admitted to the bar in 1813.

During the War of 1812, Dallas joined a volunteer company. Then, at the insistence of his father, he journeyed to Russia on a peace mission, serving as private secretary to Albert Gallatin, United States minister to Russia. Later in the war, Gallatin sent him to London to arrange a peace conference between the United States and Great Britain. Dallas returned to the United States in 1814 with the first British peace offer.

After assisting his father in the Treasury Department for a while, Dallas went back to Philadelphia to practice law. He soon was recognized as a brilliant young lawyer. On May 23, 1816, at the age of twenty-four, he married Sophia Nickin.

Dallas became active in Pennsylvania politics, and in 1828 was elected mayor of Philadelphia. In 1831, at the age of thirty-nine, he was chosen to fill a vacant seat in the United States Senate. He served there until 1833, when, declining reelection, he returned to Pennsylvania. He then was appointed attorney general of Pennsylvania. In 1837, President Martin Van Buren appointed him minister to Russia. He held this post through July of 1839, and then resumed the practice of law, which he loved.

In 1844 the Democratic national convention nominated James K. Polk of Tennessee for President and Dallas for Vice-President. In the election that followed, Polk and Dallas defeated the Whig candidates, Henry Clay and Theodore Frelinghuysen.

Dallas proved to be a good Vice-President. He got along well with President Polk, who consulted him frequently and asked his advice on important issues. Because of his dignity, courtesy, fairness, and wealth of knowledge, Dallas is said to have been one of the best presiding officers of the Senate. The tariff act of 1846 was passed because of his tie-breaking vote. Voting in favor of this act took great political courage, because his home state opposed it. Dallas felt that as Vice-President he represented all the states, not just his own, and that he had no right to use his vote to counteract the will of the majority of the people.

After retiring from the Vice-Presidency in 1849, Dallas resumed his law practice. In 1856 President Franklin Pierce appointed him minister to Great Britain, where he served until 1861. He died in Philadelphia on December 31, 1864, at seventy-two years of age, and was buried in St. Peter's Churchyard in that city. Dallas County, in Texas, is named after him.

Millard Fillmore

MILLARD FILLMORE, the twelfth Vice-President of the United States, was the second to succeed to the Presidency upon the death of a President. Fillmore was born on January 7, 1800, in a log cabin built by his father and uncle in a forest in Cayuga County, New York. He was the second of nine children. He grew up on his father's farm and received little formal education, attending school only three months of the year. One of his teachers, Abigail Powers, the daughter of a Baptist minister, later became his wife. In 1814, Fillmore became an apprentice to a wool carder and clothmaker. Resenting the harsh treatment given him, he bought his freedom for thirty dollars in 1819, and walked about one hundred miles back to his home.

When he was eighteen, Fillmore began to read law in the office of Judge Walter Wood. He continued the study of the law in Buffalo after his family moved there in 1820. During this period he also taught school in order to make ends meet. In 1823 he was admitted to the bar. He practiced law in East Aurora, New York, until 1830, when he moved to Buffalo. He and Abigail had been married on February 5, 1826. They had two children, a son and a daughter.

Fillmore was regarded as one of the great lawyers in New York. He became active in politics, and from 1828 to 1831 served in the New York State Assembly. In 1832 he was elected to the United States House of Representatives, where he served four terms. Fillmore became one of the leaders of the Whig party, and between 1841 and 1843, served as chairman of the House Ways and Means Committee. In 1844 he ran for governor of New York but was defeated by a narrow margin. Three years later he was elected first comptroller (public official in charge of accounts and spending) of New York State.

In 1848 the Whig national convention nominated General Zachary Taylor for President and Fillmore for Vice-President. They were elected and were inaugurated on March 5, 1849 (March 4 fell on a Sunday). One year and four months later, on July 9, 1850, President Taylor died. The following day Fillmore took the oath of office as President. The main event of Fillmore's Presidency was the passage of the Compromise of 1850. Fillmore's support of the Compromise of 1850 and of the Fugitive Slave Law averted civil war for ten years, but he lost much northern support, and with it, his chance for a Presidential term in his own right. His wife Abigail is said to have established the White House Library.

In 1852, Fillmore sought the Whig nomination for President, but it went instead to General Winfield Scott. Four years later both the Whig party and the American ("Know-Nothing") party nominated him for President, but the Democrat, James Buchanan, was elected.

Less than a month after his retirement from the Presidency, Fillmore's wife died. Fillmore practiced law in Buffalo and served as chancellor of the University of Buffalo, which he had helped to establish. In 1858 he married a widow, Caroline Carmichael McIntosh. He died in Buffalo on March 8, 1874, at the age of seventy-four, and was buried in Forest Lawn Cemetery in Buffalo, New York.

William Rufus DeVane King

WILLIAM R. D. KING, the thirteenth Vice-President of the United States, was the third to die in office. He was the only Vice-President to take the oath of office on foreign soil.

Born of Irish and Hungarian ancestry on April 7, 1786, in Sampson County, North Carolina, King graduated from the University of North Carolina in 1803. He then studied law, and in 1806 was admitted to the bar and began to practice. That same year he became a member of the North Carolina legislature, in which he served through 1809. In 1810, at the age of twenty-four, he was elected to the United States House of Representatives. When the new Congress met, King was twenty-five years old and was therefore qualified to serve. He resigned from the House in 1816, when President James Madison appointed him secretary of the United States legation in Naples, Italy. Later that year he was transferred to St. Petersburg, Russia. Upon his return to the United States in 1818, he bought a cotton plantation in Alabama, which was then a territory. In 1819, when Alabama was admitted to the Union, King was elected to the United States Senate, thus becoming one of the two first senators from Alabama.

King spent over twenty-four consecutive years in the Senate. He was president pro tempore of the Senate from 1836 to 1841. Considered its great parliamentarian, he was frequently called upon to interpret Senate rules. In 1844 he resigned from the Senate to become minister to France, but in 1848 he was appointed to fill an unexpired term in the Senate. He was reelected for a full term in 1849 and served until December 20, 1852. He was at this time the oldest member of the Senate, and because of his age and the length of his service, he has at times been called "the father of the United States Senate."

The election of King as Vice-President of the United States in 1852 on the Democratic ticket (under Franklin Pierce) meant the realization of a hope that he had long held. It came too late, however, for at the time of his election he was nearly sixty-seven years old, and his health was failing rapidly. By December 20, 1852, less than two months after the election, his health had become so poor that he resigned from the Senate and went to Cuba, where he hoped to recover from his illness — tuberculosis. But he continued to grow weaker, and by February, 1853, he felt that he would not be able to go to Washington to take the oath of office as Vice-President. On March 2, 1853, a special act was passed by Congress, permitting him to take the oath in Cuba.

The oath was administered to him on March 24, 1853, by William L. Sharkey, United States consul at Havana. In April, 1853, King decided to return to the United States for his last days. He left Cuba on April 7, and on April 17 he reached his home in Selma, Alabama, where he died the following evening. He is buried in the City Cemetery in Selma.

King had remained a bachelor all his life and had served nearly fifty years in public life, almost twenty-nine of them in the Senate. In his message to Congress the December following King's death, President Pierce said, "His loss to the country . . . has been justly regarded as irreparable."

John Cabell Breckinridge

JOHN C. BRECKINRIDGE, the fourteenth Vice-President of the United States, was the youngest man ever to take the oath of office as Vice-President. He was born on January 21, 1821, near Lexington, Kentucky, into one of the oldest families in the state. After graduating from Centre College in Danville, Kentucky, at eighteen, he attended the College of New Jersey. His father was a well-known lawyer who died at thirty-four years of age. Breckinridge studied law at Transylvania University in Kentucky, and practiced first in Frankfort, Kentucky, then in Burlington, Iowa, and finally in Lexington. He married Mary C. Burch of Scott County in 1843.

During the Mexican War, Breckinridge served as a major in a volunteer regiment. In 1849, at the age of twenty-eight, he became a member of the Kentucky legislature. Two years later he was elected to the United States House of Representatives, where he served two terms. He refused a third term, declined President Pierce's offer to make him minister to Spain, and returned to the practice of law. In 1856 the Democratic party convention nominated Breckinridge, a Southerner, for Vice-President on a ticket with James Buchanan. Buchanan, a bachelor, was sixty-five years of age, which made him older than any previous President except Harrison. Because Breckinridge was very popular in Kentucky, it was thought he would be able to swing his state's votes to the Democratic party. As hoped, Buchanan and Breckinridge won the election. On March 4, 1857, Breckinridge was sworn in as Vice-President, at thirty-six years of age.

As Vice-President, Breckinridge was an able and well-liked presiding officer of the Senate during the trying years leading up to the Civil War. In 1860 the Independent Democratic party (the southern proslavery wing of the Democratic party) nominated him for President. Abraham Lincoln won the election.

Returning to the Senate in 1861, Breckinridge served there a short while, then resigned to join the Confederate Army. He was made a brigadier general and was later promoted to the rank of major general. He served in many of the campaigns of the Civil War, including several with Generals Robert E. Lee and Jubal Early.

During the latter part of the Civil War, Breckinridge was made Secretary of War of the Confederacy. When the war ended and the Confederacy collapsed, he went to Europe. In 1869 he returned to Kentucky and resumed the practice of law in Lexington. He died there on May 17, 1875, at the age of fifty-four. In 1886 the state erected a statue of him in Lexington, where he is buried.

Hannibal Hamlin

HANNIBAL HAMLIN, the fifteenth Vice-President of the United States, was born in Paris Hill, Maine, on August 27, 1809. The son of a doctor-farmer, he was educated in a local school until the age of twelve, then attended and was graduated from Hebron Academy, where he was known as one of the most diligent students. At sixteen, he had to interrupt his plans for a college education to work on his father's farm. He also taught in a district school.

Having saved some money, Hamlin began to study law, but his studies were again interrupted when his father died suddenly. He returned to work on the farm and took care of his mother. Two years later (1830) he and a friend, Horatio King, bought the local newspaper, the *Jeffersonian*, but Hamlin sold his share to King and resumed the study of law. In 1833, at twenty-four years of age, he was admitted to the bar. Later the same year he married Sarah J. Emery, the daughter of his first legal opponent, Judge Stephen A. Emery. After Sarah died in 1855, he married her half sister, Ellen V. Emery. Hamlin had one child, a son, Charles.

Turning to politics, Hamlin was elected to the Maine legislature in 1836. He served there for five successive terms, during most of which he was speaker. In 1842 he was elected to Congress. From the outset of his congressional career he expressed his opposition to slavery. After one speech, John Quincy Adams, who was then serving in

40

Congress following his term as President, praised Hamlin for his antislavery views. Because of these views much attention was drawn to Hamlin. He was reelected by a large majority in 1844. In 1846 he was an unsuccessful candidate for the United States Senate, but in 1848 he was chosen by the Maine legislature to fill the seat of a senator who had died. When that term expired, Hamlin was elected to a full term. In the Senate he continued his outspoken criticism of slavery. This made him unpopular with certain Democrats, and finally, in 1856, he resigned from the Democratic party and joined the Republican party.

Shortly thereafter, the Republicans nominated him for governor of Maine. He was elected by a large margin, thus becoming the first Republican governor of the state. He had served only a few weeks when in February, 1857, he resigned in order to return to the Senate for another term.

In May, 1860, the Republican party convention nominated Abraham Lincoln of Illinois for President and Hamlin for Vice-President. After they were elected, Lincoln sought Hamlin's advice on appointments and other important matters. As Vice-President, Hamlin enjoyed a close relationship with Lincoln and was respected by him. He was with Lincoln at the dedication of the national cemetery at Gettysburg on November 19, 1863, when Lincoln delivered his historic Gettysburg Address.

Hamlin was not renominated for Vice-President in 1864 because it was thought that a Democrat who had remained loyal to the Union should share the ticket with Lincoln, a Republican.

After the assassination of President Lincoln in 1865, President Andrew Johnson appointed Hamlin collector of the Port of Boston. Hamlin resigned from that post in 1866. In 1869 he was reelected to the United States Senate, and he served for twelve years. In June, 1881, President James A. Garfield appointed Hamlin minister to Spain, where he served until January, 1883. He died on July 4, 1891, at the age of eighty-one, in Bangor, Maine, where he is buried. Senator Henry L. Dawes said it was characteristic of Hamlin that he wore "a black swallow-tailed coat, and . . . clung to the old fashioned stock after it had been discarded by the rest of mankind."

Andrew Johnson

ANDREW JOHNSON, the sixteenth Vice-President of the United States, was the third to succeed to the Presidency upon the death of a President. Johnson was born on December 29, 1808, in Raleigh, North Carolina, the youngest of three children. His father was a porter and constable, and his mother worked as a maid in a Raleigh tavern. When Johnson was three years old, his father died, leaving his family penniless. As a result, Johnson could not go to school. His mother did laundry and sewing to support her family. When he was thirteen, Johnson's mother apprenticed him to a tailor in Wake County, North Carolina. He taught himself to read and write in his spare time.

After two years, Johnson ran away to Laurens, South Carolina, and opened a tailor shop. In 1826 he took his mother, stepfather, and brother to Greenville, Tennessee, where he opened another tailor shop. On May 17, 1827, at the age of eighteen, he married Eliza McCardle, the daughter of a shoemaker. She became a tremendous force in his life, helping him with his reading and writing and also with his political career. They had five children.

Johnson turned to politics before his twenty-first birthday. He organized and became the leader of a workingman's party in Greenville. In 1828 he was elected to the town council. After serving on the council for three terms, he became mayor of Greenville. He served as mayor for three terms and then focused his attention on state politics. Between 1834 and 1843, Johnson served as a delegate to the state constitutional convention and as a member of each house of the Tennessee legislature. In 1843 he was elected to the United States House of Representatives, where he served until his election as governor of Tennessee in 1853. He became known as a man of integrity and principle, who championed the cause of the small farmer.

Johnson was reelected governor in 1855. In 1857 he was elected to the United States Senate. At the outbreak of the Civil War, Tennessee, with other Southern states, seceded from the Union. Johnson was the only Southern senator who refused to secede with his state. In December, 1860, he made a moving speech in the Senate for unity, saying of President-elect Lincoln:

"I voted against him; I spoke against him; I spent my money to defeat him; but still I love my country; I love the Constitution; I intend to insist upon its guarantees."

In 1862 Johnson demonstrated his loyalty to the government by serving as military governor of Tennessee. In 1864, Lincoln was anxious to have a prominent Union Democrat as his Vice-Presidential running mate. Johnson was nominated. On April 14, 1865, less than forty-five days after starting his second term, Lincoln was assassinated. Johnson succeeded to the Presidency. It became his task to restore the Southern states to the Union. No President ever had a more difficult job. Johnson stood by Lincoln's program of restoring the South peacefully and without severe punishment, doing what he thought was right. He had to deal with what was perhaps the most hostile Congress in American history. His struggle with Congress reached its peak in 1868, when he was impeached by the House of Representatives for removing a Cabinet officer without the Senate's consent — a right clearly belonging to the President. The Senate, by only one vote, acquitted Johnson.

Johnson retired from the Presidency in 1869, an embittered man. In 1874 he was reelected to the Senate, but died of a paralytic stroke on July 31, 1875. He was buried in Greenville, Tennessee, with a copy of the Constitution under his head.

Schuyler Colfax

SCHUYLER COLFAX, the seventeenth Vice-President of the United States, was born in New York City on March 23, 1823. His father died before he was born. He attended the New York public schools and then worked as a clerk for his stepfather. In 1836, when he was thirteen, his family moved to New Carlisle, Indiana, where he worked as a clerk in a store. In 1841 his stepfather became auditor of St. Joseph County and made young Colfax his assistant. Colfax served for a while as a clerk in the state senate and as a correspondent for the *Indiana State Journal*. He married Evelyn Clark of New York on October 10, 1844. She died in 1863.

Colfax studied law, but was never admitted to the bar. In 1845 he founded the *St. Joseph Valley Register,* a weekly newspaper that became very influential in Indiana. He was a member of the Indiana state constitutional convention in 1850, and in 1854 he was elected to the United States House of Representatives. He was reelected six consecutive times, holding office from 1855 to 1869. His popularity and ability won him election as speaker of the House. He held this position from before the Civil War until his retirement from the House in 1869.

In 1868 the Republican party convention nominated Colfax for Vice-President on a ticket with General Ulysses S. Grant. The Republican candidates were only one year apart in age, and were remarkably alike in physical appearance, being of about the same height and weight and both having beards. In personality, however, they were quite different. Grant had been toughened by the hardships of war, while Colfax had a gentle manner and always sought to avoid quarrels.

Grant and Colfax defeated the Democratic candidates, Horatio Seymour and Francis Preston Blair, Jr. On November 18, 1868, while he was Vice-President-elect, Colfax, a widower, remarried. His bride was Ellen W. Wade, the niece of Senator Benjamin F. Wade of Ohio, a runner-up for the Vice-Presidential nomination. Wade was one of the most radical of the Republicans who had sought to impeach President Johnson. Colfax and his second wife had six children.

Upon leaving the Vice-Presidency on March 4, 1873, Colfax retired from politics and made his living by lecturing. He died on January 13, 1885, in Mankato, Minnesota, at the age of sixty-one. He is buried in South Bend, Indiana.

Henry Wilson

HENRY WILSON, the eighteenth Vice-President of the United States, was the fourth to die in office. Born Jeremiah Jones Colbath on February 16, 1812, in Farmington, New Hampshire, he was the son of a day laborer in a sawmill. His parents were so poor that at the age of ten he became an indentured worker on a neighboring farm. He was permitted to go to school one month each year. Wilson spent his free time reading borrowed books. By the time he was twenty he had read nearly one thousand volumes, mostly English and American history and biography. When he reached manhood, he had his name changed to Henry Wilson. He took his new name from one of the biographies he had read.

In 1833, after failing to find a job in any of the neighboring towns, Wilson walked more than one hundred miles to Natick, Massachusetts, where he took up shoemaking and established his own business. This was the origin of his nickname, "the Natick Cobbler," which remained with him the rest of his life. Failing health forced him to sell his business, and he went to Virginia to recuperate. While there he visited Washington, D. C., and listened to the debates over slavery. Convinced of the evils of slavery, he decided to devote the rest of his life to the cause of emancipation.

Upon returning to New Hampshire, Wilson entered school, but was forced to leave when he ran out of money. He returned to Natick and taught school for a while. In 1838 he returned to making shoes and gradually built his business into a thriving enterprise. In 1840 he married Harriet Malvina Howe. They had one son.

In 1840, Wilson was elected to the Massachusetts legislature as a representative from Natick. Reelected several times, he worked hard for his party and became well known for his antislavery speeches.

When the Whig party convention of 1848 failed to take a stand on the Wilmot Proviso (which forbade slavery in any territory acquired from Mexico), Wilson called those favoring the proviso to a separate convention. This was the beginning of the Free Soil party.

Wilson served as president of the Massachusetts state senate in 1851 and 1852, and in 1852 he was made president of the Free Soil national convention. The following year he was a delegate to the Massachusetts constitutional convention and an unsuccessful candidate for governor of Massachusetts on the Free Soil ticket.

In 1855, when one of the United States senators from Massachusetts resigned, Wilson was elected to finish his term. He was reelected and remained a member of the Senate until 1873, when he became Vice-President during Grant's second term. One of the founders of the Republican party, he actively campaigned for Lincoln's election in 1860.

At the end of the Civil War Wilson was more deeply concerned than ever with the rights of Negroes, and worked on their behalf in the Senate. When the Republicans renominated Grant for President in 1872, Wilson was nominated for Vice-President. That November, Grant and Wilson were elected. It is said that Wilson was so poor that he had to borrow money from a friend to take care of his inauguration expenses. During his Vice-Presidency, Wilson spent a good deal of time writing his major work, *A History of the Rise and Fall of the Slave Power in America* (three volumes). On November 10, 1875, Wilson suffered a paralytic stroke in the Capitol and a bed was set up for him in the Vice-President's office there. He seemed to improve during the next week and was making plans to go home as soon as he had recovered sufficiently. Then, at 7:20 A.M. on November 22, he suffered another stroke and died almost instantly. He was buried in Old Dell Park Cemetery in Natick, Massachusetts.

William Almon Wheeler

THE NINETEENTH Vice-President of the United States, William A. Wheeler, was born in Malone, Franklin County, New York, on June 30, 1819. His grandfathers were Vermont pioneers and soldiers in the Revolutionary War. In 1827, Wheeler's father, a young lawyer, died without leaving an estate. His mother had to support herself and her children by boarding students attending Franklin Academy.

Wheeler worked his way through Franklin Academy, and then studied at the University of Vermont, still working to pay his way. After two years he had to leave the university because of financial difficulties and eye trouble. He began to study law, and in 1845 was admitted to the bar. He married Mary King on September 17, 1845. The following year he was elected district attorney of Franklin County, New York. He held that position until 1849, when he was elected to the New York State legislature.

In 1858, Wheeler was elected to the New York State Senate, and two years later was elected to the United States House of Representatives, where he served for one term. In 1867 and 1868 he presided over the New York constitutional convention. He was again elected to Congress in 1868, and served another four terms. While in Congress, Wheeler was the author of the Wheeler Adjustment, a compromise settling a disputed election in Louisiana. He was regarded as a man of high integrity. The "salary grab" act of 1873, which increased the salaries of many government officials, was passed over his opposition. Wheeler returned his salary increase to the treasury.

In 1876 the Republican party convention nominated Governor Rutherford B. Hayes of Ohio for President. To balance the ticket geographically, Wheeler was nominated for Vice-President. Hayes and Wheeler defeated the Democrats, Samuel Jones Tilden and Thomas Andrews Hendricks, in a close election. Wheeler's political views were similar to those of Hayes and they became good friends. As Vice-President, Wheeler was a good presiding officer of the Senate. Poor health forced him to retire from politics after his one term as Vice-President, and he returned to his law practice. He died in Malone, New York, on June 4, 1887, at the age of sixty-seven. He is buried in Malone.

Chester Alan Arthur

CHESTER A. ARTHUR, the twentieth Vice-President of the United States, was the fourth to succeed to the Presidency upon the death in office of the President. He was born in Fairfield, Franklin County, Vermont, on October 5, 1830. He was the fifth of nine children and the first son of a Baptist clergyman who had emigrated to the United States from County Antrim, Ireland. Arthur attended the New York public schools. He then entered Union College in Schenectady and before long became a member of almost every club on the campus. Arthur was graduated with honors from Union College in 1848. He then taught school for a brief while and became principal of an academy in North Pownal, Vermont. During this period, Arthur studied law, and in 1854 was admitted to the New York bar.

While still very young, Arthur handled several famous cases and was soon recognized as an excellent lawyer. One of the cases involved the question of whether some slaves brought into New York by their owner were free, since New York had abolished slavery. Arthur defended the slaves and won the case.

In 1859, at the age of twenty-nine, he married Ellen Lewis Herndon, the daughter of a Navy captain. They had two sons and a daughter, but one son died in infancy.

During his early years as a lawyer Arthur participated in local New York City politics. He also joined the militia. In 1860 he was appointed engineer-in-chief of the New York State militia, with the rank of brigadier general. In 1862 he became quartermaster-general, but in the following year he resumed the practice of the law.

From 1863 to 1871 Arthur practiced law and again took an active part in New York City politics. In 1871, President Ulysses S. Grant appointed him collector of customs for the port of New York. He served in this post until 1878, when he once again returned to the practice of law.

In 1880, Arthur attended the Republican national convention as a delegate from New York. He favored the nomination of former President Grant for another term. When Grant lost to James A. Garfield, Arthur was chosen to run as Garfield's Vice-President in order to unite the two factions of the Republican party.

On July 2, 1881, less than four months after becoming President, Garfield was shot. He wavered between life and death for eighty days, and then on September 19, 1881, he died. Arthur, at the age of fifty, became the twenty-first President of the United States, the first born in Vermont.

Arthur was a conscientious and personable President, and he won the respect of many Americans. One of his main accomplishments was the bringing about of needed civil service reform. He signed into law the Pendleton Civil Service Act of 1883.

When Arthur did not obtain the Republican nomination for President in 1884, he returned to his law practice in New York. He died of a cerebral hemorrhage on November 18, 1886, and was buried in Rural Cemetery, Albany, New York.

Thomas Andrews Hendricks

THOMAS A. HENDRICKS, the twenty-first Vice-President and the fifth to die in office, was born on September 7, 1819, in Muskingum County, Ohio. Hendricks' father was a farmer and a surveyor. In 1820, Hendricks' family moved to a farm in Indiana. He received his early education at Shelby County Seminary and Greenburg Academy, then attended Hanover College. Following his graduation in 1841, he studied law, first in Shelbyville, and later under his uncle, Judge Alexander Thompson, in Chambersburg, Pennsylvania. He was admitted to the bar in 1843. Also in that year, he married Eliza C. Morgan of Northbend, Ohio. Their only child died at the age of three.

A successful lawyer and an excellent public speaker, Hendricks entered politics in 1848 and was elected to the Indiana legislature. In 1850 he served as a member of the Indiana constitutional convention, and in 1851 he was elected to the United States House of Representatives.

Shortly after Hendricks' second term in Congress expired, President Franklin Pierce appointed him commissioner of the General Land Office. He performed his duties well in that position and made a national reputation for himself. He resigned in 1859 because of differences with President Buchanan. He ran for governor of Indiana in 1860 and lost, but in 1863 he won election to the United States Senate. Although Hendricks soon became a prominent member of the Democratic opposition, he remained a model of courtesy. He favored large appropriations to carry out the Civil War, supported President Andrew Johnson's reconstruction program, and voted for acquittal at Johnson's trial in the Senate. In 1868, while still a senator, he was an unsuccessful candidate for the Democratic Presidential nomination and also for the governorship of Indiana. He was to be a candidate for the Democratic Presidential nomination every four years, with one exception, from 1868 until his death. When his term as senator expired, Hendricks returned to his law practice in Indiana.

In 1872, Hendricks was elected governor of Indiana. When Horace Greeley, the Democratic candidate for President, died several weeks after the election, Hendricks was given forty-two of the sixty-six electoral votes won by Greeley. In 1876, Hendricks received the Democratic nomination for Vice-President on the ticket with Samuel J. Tilden. Although they won a majority of the popular votes, they lost the disputed election to Rutherford B. Hayes and William A. Wheeler. The election was decided by an electoral commission consisting of eight Republicans and seven Democrats. From 1876 to 1884, Hendricks practiced law in Indianapolis and took an active part in the affairs of his church. Hendricks again received the Democratic nomination for Vice-President, this time on a ticket with Grover Cleveland in 1884. They defeated the Republicans, but by then Hendricks was sixty-five years of age. After serving only eight months of his term, he died suddenly in Indianapolis, Indiana, on November 25, 1885. He is buried in Indianapolis.

Levi Parsons Morton

THE TWENTY-SECOND Vice-President of the United States, Levi P. Morton, was born in Shoreham, Vermont, on May 16, 1824. His father was a minister and a descendant of George Morton, one of the earliest settlers of Plymouth. His mother was a descendant of Joseph Parsons, one of the founders of the early settlements at Springfield and Northampton.

Morton, the youngest son in his family, did not receive much education. At fourteen he began working in a store in return for room, board, and a small salary. By 1843 he had his own mercantile business in Hanover, New Hampshire, and before long was a prosperous businessman.

When he was twenty-five, Morton went to work for J. M. Beebe and Company, a famous Boston cotton firm. Two years later he was made a junior partner. It was here that he met Junius Spencer Morgan, a partner in the firm, who was the father of J. Pierpont Morgan. In 1854, Morton became manager of a branch of the Beebe Company in New York. He then set up a wholesale dry goods business of his own — Morton, Grinnell & Company, which was forced into bankruptcy by the Civil War. Morton later rebuilt the business and was able to pay his old debts, including the interest. He married Lucy Young Kimball of Long Island on October 15, 1856. She died in 1871, and on February 12, 1873, he married Anna Livingston Read Street. Morton and his second wife had five children.

In 1863, Morton entered the banking business. It was partly because of his association with Junius Spencer Morgan that he soon became one of the foremost international bankers, with offices in the United States and London.

In 1876 Morton ran for Congress from New York City, but was defeated by the incumbent (the person already holding office). In 1878, at the age of fifty-five, he was elected to Congress by a sizable majority. During his term he dedicated himself to improving the life of the worker. In 1880, Morton had an opportunity to run for Vice-President, but he declined. When Garfield was elected President, he offered to appoint Morton as Secretary of the Navy. Morton asked instead to be made minister to England or France. He was appointed minister to France and served in that position with distinction. He was influential and very well liked.

In 1885, when his appointment expired, he was defeated for a seat in the United States Senate. He then bought an estate near Poughkeepsie, New York, where he raised dairy cows. In 1887 he again ran for the Senate but withdrew when a deadlock resulted. The following year the Republican party nominated him for Vice-President on a ticket with Benjamin Harrison. They defeated President Grover Cleveland and Allen G. Thurman.

Morton enjoyed the prestige of the second-highest office of the nation. He was on friendly terms with Harrison and was a dignified, courteous, and well-liked president of the Senate. When his term ended, all the senators — Republicans and Democrats — gave him a farewell dinner. After he retired as Vice-President, Morton was elected governor of New York and served from 1895 to 1897. He then returned to banking, and in 1899 founded the Morton Trust Company. He died at his country estate, Ellerslie, near Rhinecliff on the Hudson, on May 16, 1920 — his ninety-sixth birthday. Three daughters survived him.

Adlai Ewing Stevenson

ADLAI E. STEVENSON, the twenty-third Vice-President of the United States, was born in Christian County, Kentucky, on October 23, 1835. His family came from Ulster, Ireland, and settled in North Carolina, where his father was born. Stevenson's father was a slave owner and small farmer. The Stevenson family moved to Bloomington, Illinois, in 1852. Stevenson taught country school and attended Illinois Wesleyan University. Later he attended Centre College in Kentucky, where he met his future wife, Letitia Green, the daughter of the president of the college. The death of his father forced Stevenson to leave Centre before graduation. He then studied law and was admitted to the bar, and in 1858 he opened his law office in Metamora, Illinois. He served in the courts of Illinois and later was a state attorney there. In 1869, Stevenson formed a law partnership in Bloomington with Judge James S. Ewing. The partnership lasted for twenty-five years.

In 1874, Stevenson, a Democrat, was elected to Congress from a heavily Republican district, defeating a well-known Republican leader. He was defeated for reelection in 1876, but won again in 1878. In 1885 he was appointed Assistant Postmaster General in President Cleveland's first administration.

In 1892, when Cleveland was nominated by the Democratic convention for a second term as President, Stevenson was nominated for the Vice-Presidency. A westerner and a supporter of "soft money" (the free coinage of silver), Stevenson was chosen to balance Cleveland, an easterner and a believer in "sound money" (the continuation of the gold standard). They won.

As Vice-President, Stevenson was friendly with Cleveland, but they disagreed on various issues. Stevenson was a well-liked president of the Senate.

In 1896, when the Democratic party nominated William Jennings Bryan for President, Stevenson was not renominated for Vice-President. Four years later, however, he received the Vice-Presidential nomination on the Democratic ticket with Bryan, but they were defeated by William McKinley and Theodore Roosevelt. Stevenson met defeat once more when he ran for the governorship of Illinois in 1908. In 1909 a book he wrote, *Something of Men I Have Known,* was published. He died in Chicago on June 14, 1914, at the age of seventy-eight. He is buried in Bloomington, Illinois. His grandson, Adlai E. Stevenson, was an unsuccessful Democratic candidate for President in 1952 and in 1956, and later served his nation with great dignity as ambassador to the United Nations.

Garret Augustus Hobart

GARRET A. HOBART, the twenty-fourth Vice-President of the United States and the sixth to die in office, was born on June 3, 1844, in Long Branch, New Jersey. His father was of English descent, and his mother, Dutch and French Huguenot. The son of a schoolteacher, Hobart was a bright and friendly boy. When he was sixteen, he entered Rutgers College, where he was a student of unusual ability. After graduating in 1863, with honors in mathematics and English, Hobart spent a short time teaching school. He then began to study law in Paterson, New Jersey, under Socrates Tuttle, a lawyer and longtime friend of his father's. In 1866, at the age of twenty-two, Hobart received his license to practice law.

On July 21, 1869, Hobart married Jennie Tuttle, the daughter of his law teacher. This was the beginning of a very happy marriage. They had two children. Hobart was chosen counsel for the city of Paterson in 1871, and in 1872, at twenty-eight, he was elected to the state assembly. He was reelected the following year, and in 1874 was chosen speaker. From 1876 to 1882 he served in the state senate, holding the position of president of the senate in 1881 and 1882. He was the first man in New Jersey history ever to serve as both speaker of the assembly and president of the senate.

In 1884, Hobart, who had become one of New Jersey's most prominent Republicans, was elected a member of the Republican national committee. In the same year he lost a race for the United States Senate. Apart from politics, Hobart was very successful, both

58

as a businessman and as an adviser to several large corporations.

In 1896 the New Jersey Republican convention unanimously recommended Hobart for the Vice-Presidential nomination on a ticket with William McKinley. When the national Republican convention met in St. Louis, this was the ticket that was nominated. Campaigning against William Jennings Bryan and Arthur Sewall, Hobart carried on a vigorous, persuasive, and successful campaign and became the first Vice-President from New Jersey.

His relationship with President McKinley was one of the closest and warmest that has ever existed between a President and Vice-President. They met frequently both for social visits and for serious conferences on national affairs.

In 1899, Hobart's health had become poor. At the end of the Senate session he collapsed from exhaustion, and during the summer of that year he grew weaker. He died in his sleep at 8:30 A.M., November 21, 1899, at the age of fifty-five. Survived by his wife and one child, he was buried in Cedar Lawn Cemetery in Paterson, New Jersey. In 1903 a bronze statue was erected to his memory on the plaza of City Hall in Paterson.

Although Hobart had served only two years and eight months as Vice-President, he had given new dimension to that office. As Senator Henry Cabot Lodge of Massachusetts then said:

"He restored the Vice-Presidency to its proper position, and lifted it up before the people to the dignity and importance which it merits. . . . Without knowing exactly why, people suddenly came to realize there was a Vice-President of the United States, that he held the second position in the government, and that with the exception of the President he was the only man in the country holding office by the vote of the entire people. . . ."

With Hobart in office the decline of the Vice-Presidency ceased, and the dawn of the twentieth century brought the restoration of the prestige of the Vice-Presidency.

Theodore Roosevelt

THEODORE ROOSEVELT was the twenty-fifth Vice-President of the United States, the fifth to succeed to the Presidency, the fourth to be elected President, and the first of those who succeeded to the Presidency to be elected President in his own right.

Roosevelt was born on October 27, 1858, in his family's home in New York City. He was the second of four children and the son of Theodore Roosevelt, a prosperous glass merchant. As a boy, Roosevelt suffered from ill health. By using iron bars and other accessories, he succeeded in building up his body. He entered Harvard College in 1876 and graduated on June 30, 1880, at the age of twenty-one. Later that year Roosevelt married Alice Hathaway Lee of Chestnut Hill, Massachusetts, and entered Columbia Law School. He did not enjoy the study of law, and therefore left law school. From 1882 to 1884 he served in the New York assembly, where he earned a good reputation because of his battle against corruption.

In 1884, two days after the birth of his first child, his wife died of Bright's disease. Her death came only a few hours after the death of his mother. Heartbroken, Roosevelt left New York for the Dakota territory and spent the next few years working and writing on his ranch there. He returned to New York City in 1886, and unsuccessfully ran for mayor. On December 2, 1886, he married Edith Kermit Carow, a childhood friend. They had five children.

Roosevelt served as a member of the United States Civil Service Commission from 1889 to 1895. In 1897 he became Assistant Secretary of the Navy. When the Spanish-American War broke out, he resigned from this post and organized the First United States Volunteer Cavalry, known as Roosevelt's Rough Riders. In the battle of San Juan Hill he personally led the Rough Riders, and contributed significantly to a successful and early conclusion of the war. He was promoted to the rank of colonel for his outstanding leadership, and became a national hero.

Upon returning to New York, Roosevelt again turned to the world of politics, and was elected governor in 1898. He served as governor until 1900, when he was nominated for Vice-President on the Republican ticket headed by President William McKinley. The election of 1900 brought them an overwhelming victory. Roosevelt began his duties as Vice-President on March 4, 1901.

On September 14, 1901, following the assassination of President McKinley, Roosevelt was sworn in as President. He was then only forty-two years of age, the youngest person ever to become President of the United States.

Roosevelt was a colorful and forceful President. So effective was his leadership that he was unanimously nominated for President by the Republican party in 1904. Elected by more than two and one-half million votes, the largest majority any President had received up to that time, he continued to give the country outstanding leadership. In 1908, Roosevelt decided not to seek reelection, following the precedent whereby no President served more than two terms.

Upon his retirement from the Presidency, Roosevelt left for Africa on a big-game hunting and scientific expedition. When he failed to obtain the Republican party nomination for President in 1912, he organized the Progressive, or Bull Moose, party and became its candidate for President. He received more popular votes than the Republican nominee, President William H. Taft, but fewer than the Democratic candidate, Woodrow Wilson. This was Roosevelt's last venture in politics. On January 6, 1919, at the age of sixty, he died, and was buried in Oyster Bay, New York.

Charles Warren Fairbanks

CHARLES W. FAIRBANKS, the twenty-sixth Vice-President of the United States, was born May 11, 1852, in a one-room log farmhouse near Unionville Centre, Union County, Ohio. As a boy, Fairbanks worked barefoot in the fields. His parents hid runaway slaves. Every day Fairbanks had to walk about a mile and a half to the local school. He worked his way through Ohio Wesleyan University and graduated in 1872. While at the university he met his future wife, Cornelia Cole, the daughter of a judge. He married her in 1874. They had four sons and a daughter.

Following his graduation from Ohio Wesleyan University, Fairbanks worked during the daytime and attended law school at night. He was admitted to the Ohio bar in 1874, but then moved to Indianapolis, Indiana, to practice law. Discovering a new field of law in railroad bankruptcies, Fairbanks became a specialist in that area and built a thriving law practice.

He also became active in Republican politics. In 1892, Fairbanks was appointed chairman of the Indiana Republican state convention. The following year he ran as a Republican for the United States

Senate but was defeated. In 1896, as a delegate to the national Republican convention, he delivered the keynote address and served as temporary chairman. In 1897, at the age of forty-five, he was elected to the United States Senate from Indiana. In the Senate he became a strong supporter of President McKinley, whom he greatly admired, and he served on important committees, including the foreign relations committee. In 1898, Fairbanks was appointed a member of the Joint High Commission to settle differences between the United States and Canada. Two years later he was a delegate to the national Republican convention and chairman of the committee that wrote the platform. In 1902 he was reelected to the Senate. At the Republican national convention of 1904, Fairbanks was chosen as Theodore Roosevelt's running mate.

As Vice-President, Fairbanks did not take an active part in the Roosevelt administration. His relations with the President, however, were good. When his term of office expired in 1909, he retired to private life, but remained an influential figure in the Republican party. In 1912, when Roosevelt ran for the Presidency on the Progressive ticket, Fairbanks supported the Republican ticket. In 1916 he aspired to the Presidential nomination, but lost it to Charles Evans Hughes. He then accepted the Republican nomination for Vice-President, but he and Hughes lost to the Democratic incumbents, Wilson and Marshall. At the time of that election he was sixty-four years of age. Fairbanks died in Indianapolis less than two years later, on June 4, 1918, at the age of sixty-six. He is buried in Indianapolis.

James Schoolcraft Sherman

JAMES S. SHERMAN, the twenty-seventh Vice-President of the United States, was the seventh to die in office. He was born in Utica, New York, on October 24, 1855. His father was a newspaper editor and a Democratic politician. Sherman's early education was in public schools and at Whitestown Seminary. In 1878 he graduated from Hamilton College and the following year received his law degree from the same school. He married Carrie Babcock of Utica in 1881, and they had three sons. In 1884, after having practiced law in Utica for a while, he was elected mayor of the city. Two years later, Sherman was elected to the House of Representatives. He served there continuously, except for two years, until 1909, when he became Vice-President.

In the House, Sherman served for many years as chairman of the committee on Indian affairs and was an influential member of the committee on finance. Loyal to the Republican organization and a hard behind-the-scenes worker, he was pleasant and popular, though firm and dignified. Sherman often relieved Speaker Thomas B. Reed in presiding over the House. Sherman's pleasantness and honesty won him many friends, and he was affectionately called "Sunny Jim."

In 1908, when Theodore Roosevelt's influence resulted in the nomination of William Howard Taft for President on the Republican ticket, Sherman was given the Vice-Presidential nomination to balance the ticket. Whereas Taft was progressive, Sherman was conservative.

Sherman did little campaigning, as his health was poor during the summer preceding the election. Taft and Sherman defeated the Democrats, William Jennings Bryan and Senator John W. Kern of Indiana, by a large margin. In 1912 Sherman was renominated for Vice-President with Taft, despite the fact that he was seriously ill. This made him the first Republican Vice-President ever to be renominated. He was not to live until election day, however. He died on October 30, 1912, six days before the election, and was buried in Utica, New York. Since the election was so close at hand, no new nomination was made. As a result, over three million people voted for a dead candidate for Vice-President. When the electoral college met, the eight electoral votes which Sherman would have received were cast for Nicholas Murray Butler, president of Columbia University, who had been designated by the Republican national committee to receive them. However, the Democratic candidates were elected.

Thomas Riley Marshall

THOMAS R. MARSHALL, the twenty-eighth Vice-President, was the fifth Vice-President to be elected twice. Marshall was born on March 14, 1854, in North Manchester, Indiana. His father was a country doctor whose parents had come to Indiana when the state was a frontier. When Marshall was a young boy his parents moved to Illinois, then to Kansas, then to Missouri, and finally back to Indiana. Marshall attended the public schools in Indiana. In 1876 he graduated from Wabash College in Crawfordsville, Indiana. After studying law in the office of Judge Walter Olds, he was admitted to the bar on March 14, 1875. For the next thirty-four years he practiced law in Columbia City, Indiana. Marshall became widely known throughout the state for his wit. On October 2, 1895, he married Lois I. Kimsey of Angola, Indiana.

In 1908, Marshall was elected governor of Indiana, his first political position. He served as governor for two terms. In 1912 he was nominated for the Vice-Presidency by the Democratic convention, which had nominated Governor Woodrow Wilson of New Jersey for President. The Democrats were victorious in the election, the first Democratic victory in twenty years.

After their inauguration, Marshall proved to be a loyal Vice-President. He supported and defended administration policies as best he could. He quickly became a popular Vice-President, mainly because of his honesty and sense of humor.

In 1916 Wilson supported Marshall's renomination, saying, "The attitude of Mr. Marshall toward the administration has been loyal and generous in the extreme. He has given me every reason to admire and trust him." Wilson and Marshall were subsequently reelected. This made Marshall the first Vice-President to be reelected since John C. Calhoun's reelection in 1828, and the first to serve two terms under the same President since Monroe's administration.

During his second term, Marshall, at Wilson's request, presided over several meetings of the Cabinet while the President attended the Paris Peace Conference in Europe. He thus became the first Vice-President since John Adams to participate in a Cabinet meeting.

When President Wilson later suffered a stroke, Marshall found himself in a delicate position. Because the Constitution was so vague, Marshall declined to act as President, although an acting President seemed to be necessary. He felt that if he attempted to act as President, he would be called a usurper and the country might be thrown into civil war. This situation emphasized the need for a constitutional amendment to define the role of a Vice-President in a case of Presidential inability.

In 1921 Marshall retired from the Vice-Presidency and returned to his law practice.

He had been one of our most popular Vice-Presidents. After his retirement he devoted a good deal of time to preparing his book, *Recollections of Thomas R. Marshall, Vice-President and Hoosier Philosopher — A Hoosier Salad,* which was published in 1925. He died on June 1, 1925, while on a business trip in Washington, D. C. He was seventy-one years old at the time of his death. He is buried in Indianapolis.

Calvin Coolidge

CALVIN COOLIDGE was the twenty-ninth Vice-President of the United States, the sixth to succeed upon the death of the President, and the fifth to be elected President in his own right.

Coolidge was born John Calvin Coolidge on July 4, 1872, in Plymouth, Vermont. His ancestors had come to America from England in the early 1600's and had settled in New England. As a boy Coolidge spent a good deal of time doing farm chores and working in his father's store. He enjoyed such activities as fishing, swimming, and exploring. In school he was conscientious and bright, and he ranked high in his class. He graduated from Black River Academy in Ludlow, Vermont, in 1890, then attended St. Johnsbury Academy, and finally entered Amherst College in 1891.

Upon his graduation with honors from Amherst in 1895, Coolidge studied law. He was admitted to the bar in Northampton, Massachusetts, in 1897. His career in politics began when he was elected a councilman of Northampton in 1899. This was followed by his election to other posts — city solicitor, clerk of the courts, member of the Massachusetts legislature, mayor of Northampton, state senator, lieutenant governor, and then governor of Massachusetts. In 1905 he married a teacher, Grace Anna Goodhue. They had two sons.

Coolidge's career in politics was marked by faithful performance of his duties and adherence to principle. He won national fame as governor for his handling of the Boston police strike of 1919. During the strike he made the famous statement that "there is no right to strike against the public safety by anybody, anywhere, any time."

At the Republican convention of 1920, the Massachusetts delegation enthusiastically supported Coolidge for the Presidential nomination, but he lost to Warren Harding. On the first ballot for the Vice-Presidency, Coolidge was nominated by a landslide. The Republicans won, with more than 60 per cent of the popular vote.

As Vice-President, Coolidge, unlike many Vice-Presidents before him, took an active part in the affairs of the administration. He was consulted by the President, gave his opinions on matters of appointments and policies, and became a regular member of the Cabinet, the first Vice-President to do so in American history. Prior to this time, the Vice-President was not included as a member of the Cabinet, following a precedent set by Thomas Jefferson. As Vice-President, Jefferson had said, "I consider my office as constitutionally confined to legislative functions, and that I could not take any part whatever in executive consultations. . . ."

On August 2, 1923, President Warren Harding died following a short illness. Coolidge, then at his father's farm in Plymouth, Vermont, received a telegram notifying him of the President's death. After reading the message he knelt in prayer. At 2:47 A.M. on August 3, Colonel John Calvin Coolidge, a notary public and magistrate of the state of Vermont, administered the Presidential oath to his son. Thus in a small parlor, by the light of a kerosene lamp, Calvin Coolidge became President of the United States.

Among the issues that Coolidge dealt with as President was the matter of government scandals. He performed his duties with his usual conscientiousness and won the respect and praise of the people. In 1924 he was easily elected President in his own right and continued to perform his duties in an effective way.

He did not seek reelection in 1928. Instead, he retired to Northampton, Massachusetts, where during the next few years he devoted a substantial amount of time to being a writer and newspaper columnist. Coolidge died of a heart attack on January 5, 1933, and was buried near Plymouth, Vermont.

Charles Gates Dawes

THE THIRTIETH Vice-President of the United States, Charles G. Dawes, was born in Marietta, Ohio, on August 27, 1865. He was a descendant of William Dawes, who, on the same night as Paul Revere, rode to warn the colonists of the approach of the British. After his graduation from Marietta College in 1884, Dawes studied law at the Cincinnati Law School. He began his practice in Lincoln, Nebraska, in 1887. On January 24, 1889, he married Caro D. Blymyer. They had four children.

In 1896, Dawes became active in politics, starting as a worker for Presidential candidate William McKinley. This led to a close friendship with McKinley, who made Dawes comptroller of the currency in the Treasury Department. He held that office from 1898 to 1902, when he returned to private business and organized the Central Trust Company of Illinois, a large bank in the Midwest.

During World War I, Dawes served as a member of President Wilson's "war cabinet," and was made general purchasing agent for the American Expeditionary Force in France, with the rank of brigadier general. He received national attention for a seven-hour speech before a congressional committee investigating wartime expenditures. His speech defended the large amount of money being spent as the only path to victory. In 1921 President Harding appointed him director of the budget. In 1923 President Coolidge appointed Dawes to a commission that was set up to investigate German finances. The commission, chaired by Dawes, established a plan (known as the Dawes Plan) that helped save Europe from economic collapse, and in 1925 Dawes was awarded the Nobel Peace Prize.

In 1924 Dawes's national reputation won him the Republican nomination for the Vice-Presidency on a ticket headed by Coolidge. He considered the nomination a great honor. The day after receiving it he said that the Vice-Presidency seemed to him "the greatest office in the world." He campaigned vigorously and he and Coolidge were elected to the nation's highest offices by a large majority.

Dawes's habit of taking an afternoon nap attracted attention during his Vice-Presidency. It was one nap in particular that made him famous. Coolidge had made a nomination for Attorney General that was vigorously opposed by the Democratic senators. During the Senate speeches Dawes went to his apartment for his customary rest. When it became apparent that the Republicans might fail to get the nomination approved, Dawes was sent for. His tie-breaking vote could do the trick. He made a dash by taxi to the Capitol, but arrived too late to cast his vote. It is said that Coolidge never forgave him. Dawes became the subject of many jokes, but by the end of his term he had established a relationship of mutual respect with the Senate. On March 2, 1929, the Senate, as a token of esteem, presented him with a silver tray engraved with the signatures of all the senators.

From the end of his term as Vice-President in 1929 until 1932, Dawes served as ambassador to Great Britain. Then for several months in 1932 he directed the Reconstruction Finance Corporation, which was set up to help banks and vital businesses recover from the depression. After that he returned to his banking business and wrote several books on banking and on his own experiences. He died in Evanston, Illinois, on April 23, 1951, at the age of eighty-five. He is buried in Chicago, Illinois.

Charles Curtis

CHARLES CURTIS, the thirty-first Vice-President of the United States, was the only man of American Indian descent to become Vice-President. He was born on January 25, 1860, on a farm near North Topeka, Shawnee County, Kansas. Curtis' mother died when he was three. From 1863 to 1866 he was cared for by his paternal grandmother. He then went to live on a Kaw Indian reservation with his maternal grandmother, Julie Gonville Papan, who was the granddaughter of a Kaw Indian chief. Curtis learned to hunt and ride, and by the time he was eight he was riding as a jockey in races at fairs.

In 1869, when the Kaw Indians were sent to the territory of Oklahoma, Curtis returned to live with his paternal grandmother. He attended school for a brief period in Topeka, then quit to concentrate on racing. His grandmother talked him into returning to school. Curtis did so, and following his graduation from elementary school he got a job on a newspaper. He also remained active in racing.

In 1876, Curtis entered high school and worked his way through school by taking odd jobs. He then began studying law, and in 1881 was admitted to the bar. Always one to remember names and faces, Curtis decided that politics was more to his liking than anything else.

On November 27, 1884, Curtis married Anna E. Baird. They had three children. In 1885 he was elected prosecuting attorney of Shawnee County. He held that office for four years, then returned to practicing law. In 1892, Curtis was elected to the House of Representatives. He served there until 1907, when he was elected by the Indiana legislature to the United States Senate. He was reelected by popular vote in 1914 and remained in the Senate until 1929, when he became Vice-President. While serving in the Senate, he acquired an excellent reputation as an organizer and as a person who could get things accomplished. He had a great deal of influence on the legislation of the times. From 1915 to 1924, Curtis served as Republican whip (assistant floor leader) of the Senate. When Senator Lodge died in 1924, Curtis was elected majority leader (floor leader) by the other Republican senators.

In 1928, President Coolidge decided not to run for another term, and Vice-President Dawes did not actively seek the Presidential nomination. Curtis sought the nomination as a "favorite son" of Kansas. His long history of party fidelity and service in Congress seemed to indicate that he had a good chance of obtaining it. The Republican convention, however, gave the nomination to Secretary of Commerce Herbert Hoover, and then nominated Curtis for Vice-President. Hoover and Curtis campaigned vigorously and were elected by an overwhelming majority.

When he entered the Vice-Presidency, Curtis was sixty-nine years of age, by no means a young man, but he had a record of long legislative experience. He was renominated for Vice-President in 1932 with Hoover, but the Republican ticket was defeated by the Democrats. When his term as Vice-President ended in March, 1933, Curtis returned to the practice of law in Washington, D. C. He died there three years later, on February 8, 1936, at the age of seventy-six. He was buried in Topeka, Kansas.

John Nance Garner

JOHN N. GARNER, the thirty-second Vice-President of the United States, was born on November 22, 1868, in a log cabin near the village of Detroit in Red River County, Texas. As a boy he worked in his uncle's store and on a farm. Although he received only four years of formal elementary education, he attended Vanderbilt University for one term and then studied law in the office of an attorney in Clarksville. In 1890 he was admitted to the Texas bar and opened an office.

For reasons of health Garner moved to Uvalde in southwestern Texas. He gradually acquired a good deal of property, including banks, businesses, houses, land, and cattle. On November 25, 1895, he married Ettie Rheiner. In 1898 he was elected to the Texas legislature, where he served two terms. He was elected to Congress in 1902 and served there until his election to the Vice-Presidency thirty years later. He did his best to represent the interests of his district in Congress, provided that they were in keeping with his idea of the national good. From the beginning of his service in the House, he set his sights on the speakership. He felt that although he might not be very brilliant or talented, he could reach that goal if he worked hard enough.

Garner first attracted national attention in 1924, when he opposed a proposed tax cut which would affect only the upper income groups. For his defense of the interests of the poorer people, he came to be regarded as a liberal. In 1928 he was chosen Democratic floor leader, and in 1931 he realized his long ambition of becoming speaker of the House of Representatives. The following year he became a candidate for the Democratic Presidential nomination. When it became apparent that Franklin Delano Roosevelt was the first choice of the Democratic convention, he released his votes in favor of Roosevelt, and in return was given the Vice-Presidential nomination. Roosevelt and Garner won.

During their first term Roosevelt consulted Garner frequently and had him attend Cabinet meetings. Garner proved to be a faithful supporter of the measures of the administration and was very persuasive when necessary. His influence in the Senate and his understanding of the men with whom he was dealing made him very effective in speeding up the Senate's consideration of measures. In his first year as Vice-President the Senate unanimously passed a resolution commending him for his "distinguished ability" as its president.

When the Democratic national convention met in 1936, Roosevelt and Garner were both renominated by acclamation, and they were reelected by an even greater margin than before. They were inaugurated on January 20, 1937.

At the Democratic convention of 1940, Roosevelt was renominated on the first ballot. Garner said that he did not wish to serve another term as Vice-President, and he retired to his home in Uvalde. One of the last acts of President John F. Kennedy on November 22, 1963, the day of his assassination, was to call former Vice-President Garner to wish him a happy ninety-fifth birthday. Garner died in Uvalde on November 7, 1967, fifteen days before his ninety-ninth birthday.

Henry Agard Wallace

HENRY A. WALLACE, the thirty-third Vice-President of the United States, was born in Adair County, Iowa, on October 7, 1888. He was raised on a farm and studied scientific farming at Iowa State College, from which he graduated in 1910. He then managed the family newspaper, *Wallace's Farmer,* which had been founded by his grandfather. The paper was later edited by his father, who served as Secretary of Agriculture under Presidents Harding and Coolidge. One of young Wallace's significant contributions to the science of farming was his development of a very good hybrid corn.

On May 30, 1914, Wallace married Ilo Browne, the daughter of an Iowa schoolteacher, merchant, and dealer in land. Wallace and his wife had two sons and a daughter. During the 1920's, Wallace became interested in the political aspects of the farm problems and engaged in lobbying for farmers' interests in Washington. His activities brought him to the attention of Governor Franklin D. Roosevelt of New York. In 1932, despite Wallace's Republican attachments, he supported Roosevelt for President. After the election, Roosevelt appointed him Secretary of Agriculture and gave him the freedom to do what he thought best in the department. Among the programs fostered by Wallace were soil conservation, controlled production, and storing of surpluses to raise prices.

76

In 1940, when Roosevelt ran for his third term, he asked Wallace to run as his Vice-President. Although he was not a regular Democrat of long standing, Wallace was popular among the farmers, trusted by the working people and minority groups, and well-liked by liberals. Eleanor Roosevelt, the President's wife, addressed the Democratic convention urging it to support Wallace. Wallace was nominated and elected Vice-President.

Wallace's Vice-Presidency was notable for the varied responsibilities he was given. One of his first assignments was to represent President Roosevelt in Mexico City at the inauguration of Avila Camacho as president of Mexico. Wallace was made a member of President Roosevelt's Cabinet, and on July 30, 1941, he became chairman of the Economic Defense Board established by the President. On August 28, 1941, the Supply Priorities and Allocations Board was created, with Wallace as its chairman. That October, the President established an advisory committee on atomic energy and made Wallace a member. In 1943, at the request of the President, Wallace undertook a goodwill tour to various Latin American countries, and in the following year he visited eastern Asia, Siberia, and China. These were the first such tours made by a Vice-President.

Although Wallace was not renominated for Vice-President in 1944, he subsequently was made Secretary of Commerce in Roosevelt's Cabinet. He resigned from this post in 1946. In 1948 he was an unsuccessful candidate for the Presidency on the Progressive party ticket. He then returned to his lifelong interest, agriculture, retiring to his farm in South Salem, New York. He died on November 18, 1965, at the age of seventy-seven. He is buried in the Glendale Cemetery in Des Moines, Iowa.

Harry S Truman

HARRY S TRUMAN was the thirty-fourth Vice-President of the United States, the seventh to become President upon the death in office of the President, and the sixth to be elected President. Born on May 8, 1884, in Lamar, Missouri, he was the oldest of three children. His father was a farmer and livestock dealer. When he was six, Truman's parents bought a farm in Independence, Missouri. As a boy Truman worked on the farm and also in a local drugstore. He attended high school in Independence and was a bright student.

Poor vision prevented Truman from receiving an appointment to the United States Military Academy at West Point, and the lack of money kept him from going to college. Disappointed, he moved to Kansas City, Missouri, and during the next five years he worked on a railroad construction crew as a timekeeper, in the mailroom of a newspaper, and in a bank, first as a clerk and then as a bookkeeper. Dissatisfied with this life, he returned to Independence in 1906 to operate the family farm.

In 1917, the United States entered World War I. Truman, who had joined the National Guard while in Kansas City, was called to active duty and sent to France as a first lieutenant with an artillery unit. His leadership and courage earned him the praise of his superiors and the respect of his men.

Discharged with the rank of major, Truman returned to the United States after the war. On June 28, 1919, he married his childhood sweeetheart, Elizabeth "Bess" Virginia Wallace, a schoolteacher and the daughter of a farmer. Their only child, Mary Margaret, was born on February 17, 1924. In 1919, Truman and a friend he had met during the war opened a men's clothing store in Kansas City, but two years later the business went into bankruptcy.

It was at this time that Truman turned to politics. In 1922, at the age of thirty-eight, he was elected a county judge of Jackson County. Although the position did not involve many judicial duties, Truman studied law at the Kansas City Law School from 1923 to 1925. He was an unsuccessful candidate for reelection as county judge in 1924, but in 1926 he was elected presiding judge of the county. He held this position until 1934, when he was elected to the United States Senate. Reelected to the Senate in 1940, he became chairman of the Special Senate Committee to investigate the National Defense Program. His exposure of corruption and waste brought him national praise. At the Democratic national convention of 1944, when Roosevelt was chosen to run for a fourth term, Truman won the Vice-Presidential nomination.

Eighty-three days after his inauguration as Vice-President, Truman received the shocking news that President Roosevelt had died. On April 12, 1945, he became the thirty-second American to be sworn in as President of the United States. It was suddenly up to him to end World War II and lead the nation through the postwar period. "I felt like the moon, the stars, and all the planets had fallen on me," he said.

Truman met the challenge — the war ended, the United Nations was born, the Truman Doctrine and the Marshall Plan were put into effect. He subsequently won the Democratic nomination in 1948 and was elected President in his own right. He declined to run for another term in 1952, and returned to his home in Independence. After the opening of the library containing his Presidential papers, in 1957 Truman turned most of his energy to the affairs of this library and to writing. Truman died on December 26, 1972, after a long illness.

Alben William Barkley

ALBEN W. BARKLEY, the thirty-fifth Vice-President of the United States, was born on November 24, 1877, in a log cabin near Lowes in Graves County, Kentucky. Raised on a tobacco farm and educated in the local schools, he worked his way through Marvin College in Kentucky. After his graduation in 1897, he went on to further studies at Emory College in Georgia and at the University of Virginia Law School.

In 1901, Barkley was admitted to the bar and began practicing law in Paducah, Kentucky. He married Dorothy Brower on June 23, 1903. They had three children. She died on March 10, 1947.

From 1905 to 1909, Barkley served as prosecuting attorney of McCracken County. He was then made judge of the county court. When Woodrow Wilson was elected President in 1912, Barkley was elected to the United States House of Representatives. He served in the House until his election to the United States Senate in 1927. He remained in the Senate until 1949.

As a senator, Barkley served on the committee on interstate and foreign commerce, where he eventually acquired a great deal of influence. He became Senate majority leader in 1937 and held that post until 1947, when the Republicans gained a majority of the

Senate seats. He then became minority leader. During this period Barkley made the keynote address at the Democratic conventions of 1932 and 1936, and was permanent chairman of the conventions of 1940 and 1944.

In 1948 he was rewarded for his long years of service to the Democratic party by being nominated for Vice-President on the ticket headed by President Truman. Barkley was almost seventy-one years old. For him the nomination came as the fulfillment of a long-held dream.

Barkley became one of the most popular Vice-Presidents in American history. He was the oldest man ever to hold the office. Affectionately called "the Veep," he had an excellent relationship with President Truman, who once referred to him as "the best Vice-President a President ever had." Truman's own experience — the vast lack of information he had when the Presidency suddenly descended upon his shoulders — led him to make Barkley a "working Vice-President." With Truman's approval, Congress passed a law making the Vice-President a member of the National Security Council. While Barkley was Vice-President, Truman decided the Vice-President should have his own flag and seal and ordered them designed. In what was described as the romance of the year, Barkley married Jane S. Hadley in St. Louis on November 18, 1949.

In 1952, Barkley sought the Democratic Presidential nomination but lost it to Governor Adlai E. Stevenson of Illinois. His age, seventy-four, was a major factor in his failure to receive the nomination. After it became evident that he would not be nominated, Barkley announced his withdrawal from the race and asked to address the convention. When he appeared, he was given an ovation that lasted nearly half an hour, and after his speech he received another ovation that lasted forty-five minutes.

Barkley was reelected to the Senate in 1954, and it was as a senator that he died on April 30, 1956, in Lexington, Virginia, at the age of seventy-eight. He is buried in Paducah, Kentucky.

Richard Milhous Nixon

RICHARD M. NIXON was the thirty-sixth Vice-President of the United States and the seventh to be elected for two terms. He was born of Quaker parents on January 9, 1913, in Yorba Linda, California. Nixon's family moved to Whittier, a community founded by Quakers. At Whittier College he excelled as a class leader, debater, and honor student. He graduated in 1934 and entered Duke University Law School on a scholarship. Following his graduation from law school in 1937, Nixon returned to Whittier and took up the practice of law. He married Thelma (Pat) Ryan, a high-school teacher, in 1940. They have two daughters.

From 1937 to 1942, Nixon practiced law. In 1942, after having worked for several months as an attorney in the Office for Emergency Management in Washington, D. C., he was commissioned a lieutenant in the United States Navy. He retired from the Navy in 1946 and ran for the House of Representatives from the Twelfth congressional district of California. After a series of debates with the incumbent, Nixon won the election. He was reelected without opposition in 1948. During his four years in the House he played a prominent part in the government's case against Alger Hiss, a former State Department official convicted of perjury.

In 1950, Nixon successfully ran for the United States Senate, and two years later he was nominated for Vice-President by the Republican national convention. At thirty-nine he was the youngest Republican nominee for that office in history. Following his inauguration as Vice-President, Nixon, with the encouragement of President Eisenhower, took on a role that made him the most active Vice-President up to that time. He served as a major spokesman for the administration, and in the President's absence, he presided over the Cabinet and the National Security Council. He also spent a considerable amount of time abroad on behalf of the President. Nixon's service as Vice-President during his two terms resulted in his nomination as Republican candidate for President in 1960. The contest between Nixon and Democratic Senator John F. Kennedy from Massachusetts was highlighted by a series of television debates. Nixon lost the election by a close margin. He was later unsuccessful in a race for governor of California.

Nixon moved to New York City and became a senior partner in a major New York law firm. He reentered politics in 1968, when he again became the Republican candidate for President. The campaign was successful, and on November 5, 1968, Richard M. Nixon became the thirty-seventh President of the United States. He and his running mate, Spiro T. Agnew, defeated Democrats Hubert Humphrey and Edmund Muskie in one of the closest elections in United States history.

Successful again in 1972, Nixon and Agnew utterly defeated Senator George S. McGovern and Sargent Shriver. Less than two years later both Nixon and Agnew had resigned their offices. Nixon's resignation, the first by a President in American history, was caused by his conduct in connection with the governmental scandal known as "Watergate." At the time of his resignation, Nixon faced almost certain impeachment by the House of Representatives and probable conviction by the Senate.

Lyndon Baines Johnson

LYNDON B. JOHNSON, the thirty-seventh Vice-President of the United States, was born on August 27, 1908, in a five-room farmhouse in Texas. He was the oldest of five children. On the day Johnson was born, his grandfather is supposed to have ridden around the countryside, saying: "A United States senator was born today."

Johnson's parents had little money. When Johnson was four, his family moved to Johnson City, where the future President started school. According to his teachers, he was a bright boy who had a great deal of energy and liked to play pranks. At high school he was president of his class and the best debater in the school. After school hours Johnson worked hard for his spending money, selling magazines, shining shoes in a barbershop, and delivering groceries.

Johnson graduated from high school in 1924 at the age of fifteen. He did not wish to go to college, despite the pleas of his mother. For a while he worked as a laborer on a road gang. In 1927 he entered Southwest Teachers College in Texas and worked his way through school. He was an active debater and served as editor of the student newspaper.

After his graduation in 1930, Johnson taught public speaking and debating at Sam Houston High School. Then, in 1931, at the age of twenty-three, he became congressional secretary to Congressman

Richard Mifflin Kleberg. When Franklin D. Roosevelt was elected President the following year, he became Johnson's hero. In November, 1934, Johnson married Claudia Alta Taylor, known by the nickname "Lady Bird." They have two children, Lynda Bird (Mrs. Charles Robb) and Luci Baines (Mrs. Patrick Nugent).

In 1935 Roosevelt appointed Johnson as head of the National Youth Administration in Texas. This program was designed to help lead the country out of the depression by finding work for young people. In 1937 he was elected to fill a vacancy in Congress caused by the death of Texas representative James P. Buchanan. He was reelected to the House five times. Johnson left Congress for seven months during World War II to serve as a lieutenant commander in the Navy. He was the first member of Congress to join the armed forces, and he received a Silver Star for his bravery on a mission in the Pacific. In 1948 Johnson won the Texas Democratic nomination for the United States Senate by eighty-seven votes, and was elected to the Senate in November. In 1951 he was elected Democratic whip of the Senate. Two years later he was elected Democratic leader of the Senate. He was reelected to the Senate in 1954, and in 1955, when the Democrats regained a majority of Senate seats, he became Senate majority leader. Johnson served as majority leader through 1960. In that year he was a candidate for the Presidential nomination. He lost the nomination to Senator John F. Kennedy, but accepted Kennedy's offer of the candidacy for Vice-President, and he was nominated. President Kennedy said, "Lyndon Johnson is the only other man I can think of with the equipment for the job of President."

For almost three years Johnson was an excellent Vice-President. When President Kennedy was assassinated on November 22, 1963, Johnson had the burdens of the Presidency placed upon him. He took the oath of office on the President's plane in Dallas, Texas.

In the months that followed, Johnson gave the country truly remarkable leadership. The people responded by electing him President in November, 1964, by the largest popular vote ever received by any President. Johnson surprised the world in 1968 by announcing that he would not run for another term. In 1969 he returned to Texas to relax and to write his memoirs. He died on January 22, 1973, and was buried at the L.B.J. ranch in Stonewall, Texas.

Hubert Horatio Humphrey

HUBERT H. HUMPHREY, the thirty-eighth Vice-President of the United States, was born on May 27, 1911, in Wallace, South Dakota. His father, a pharmacist, owned a drugstore, where the future Vice-President worked as a boy. Humphrey attended the local schools, then entered the University of Minnesota. He had to quit college during the depression in order to help out in the family drugstore. When things improved, he entered the Denver College of Pharmacy and earned a degree in pharmacy. He became a registered South Dakota pharmacist on June 20, 1933, and started work for the Humphrey Drug Company in Huron, South Dakota. In 1936 he married his childhood sweetheart, Muriel Buck, the daughter of a South Dakota farmer. They have four children.

After practicing pharmacy for a while, Humphrey came to the conclusion that he was not meant to be a pharmacist for the rest of his life. Therefore he entered the University of Minnesota in 1937 and studied political science. He graduated in 1939, and then went on to Louisiana State University, where he obtained a master's degree in political science. Following his graduation he embarked on a teaching career. He taught at Louisiana State University and at the University of Minnesota, and in 1943 and 1944 was a political science professor at Macalester College in St. Paul, Minnesota.

In 1943, Humphrey was an unsuccessful candidate for mayor of Minneapolis. In 1945, at the age of thirty-four, he was elected mayor, and during the next three years he proved to be one of the best mayors Minneapolis ever had. He instituted many reforms and new programs for the poor. Said a newspaper at the time of his election:

He seems to be a wonderful and meteoric young man, bouncy and gay, built on springs, with a fierce face and pleasant young grin. He puts firecrackers under everything.

After serving two terms as mayor, Humphrey became the first popularly elected Democratic United States senator from Minnesota. On January 3, 1949, he started his career in the Senate at the same time as Lyndon B. Johnson.

In the Senate, Humphrey sponsored legislation on a variety of matters and earned a reputation as an outstanding liberal. One of his proposals was for a peace corps. He was reelected in 1954 and 1960, and was chosen majority whip in 1961. In 1960, Humphrey was an unsuccessful candidate for the Democratic nomination for President. When Senator Kennedy became President, Humphrey became one of his strongest supporters in Congress. He was also a strong supporter of the programs of Lyndon B. Johnson after Johnson's succession to the Presidency.

It is not surprising that President Johnson recommended him to the Democratic national convention in August, 1964, as the person best equipped for the Vice-Presidency. Humphrey was endorsed as the President's running mate by acclamation. In November, 1964, he was elected the thirty-eighth Vice-President of the United States. In 1968 Humphrey lost his bid for election as United States President to Richard M. Nixon. Humphrey and his running mate, Edmund Muskie, were defeated in one of the closest Presidential elections ever held. After his service as Vice-President, Humphrey became a college professor at the University of Minnesota and Macalester College. He was re-elected to the Senate in 1970.

He died on January 13, 1978, and was buried in Lakewood Cemetery in Minneapolis.

Spiro Theodore Agnew

SPIRO T. AGNEW, the thirty-ninth Vice-President of the United States, was born on November 9, 1918, in Baltimore, Maryland. His Greek-born father, a restaurateur, changed the family name from Anagnos-topoulos to Agnew. In 1940, Agnew transferred from Johns Hopkins University to Baltimore Law School, attending classes at night and working days. During World War II he was awarded a Bronze Star. After the war Agnew returned to school as a veteran with a family. In 1942 he had married Elinor Isabel Judefind. Today they have four children.

In 1947, after receiving his law degree, Agnew and his family moved to suburban Towson. He at first worked for a law firm and then began his own practice. In Towson, Agnew switched from the Democratic to the Republican party, and worked in several election campaigns. In 1957, he became a member of the Baltimore County Zoning Board of Appeals and in 1961 was elected county executive (the equivalent of mayor) and served in that job until 1966—the first Republican to hold the post since 1895. It was in 1966 that he ran successfully for governor of Maryland.

At the 1968 Republican convention, Agnew placed Nixon's name in nomination, and Nixon named Agnew as his choice for the Vice-Presidency. On November 5, 1968, he was elected Vice-President of the United States. In 1972 he was reelected with President Nixon in the greatest landslide in United States history. On October 10, 1973, Agnew shocked the nation when he announced his resignation as Vice-President after pleading *nolo contendere* that day to a charge of federal income tax evasion.

Gerald R. Ford

On October 12, 1973 President Nixon nominated Gerald R. Ford to be our fortieth Vice-President to fill the vacancy created by the resignation of Spiro T. Agnew. On December 6, 1973 he was sworn in after having been approved by overwhelming votes in both Houses of Congress. On August 9, 1974 after Nixon's resignation, he became our thirty-eighth President. Ford was the first Vice-President to be selected under the Twenty-fifth Amendment and the ninth to succeed to the Presidency. In 1976 he ran unsuccessfully for President.

Ford was born in Omaha, Nebraska, on July 14, 1913 and, when his mother remarried, he was adopted by and took the name of her husband. During his high school days in Grand Rapids, Michigan, he waited on tables and washed dishes in a restaurant to earn money. In 1931 he entered the University of Michigan, starring on its championship football teams and being named most valuable player in 1934. He then attended Yale Law School. Afterwards, he became a practicing lawyer in Michigan. From 1942 to 1945 he served in the United States Navy. After World War II he resumed his practice of law, married Elizabeth Bloomer, and they became the parents of four children.

In 1948 Ford was elected to the House of Representatives. He was reelected twelve consecutive times. In Congress he developed a reputation for being honest, candid, hard working, and competent. In 1965 he was chosen as Minority Leader of the House of Representatives. At the time he became Vice-President, he said: "Truth is the glue on the bond that holds government together, and not only government, but civilization itself."

89

Nelson A. Rockefeller

ON AUGUST 20, 1974 President Ford nominated Nelson A. Rockefeller to be our forty-first Vice-President. He thus became the second person to be selected under the Twenty-fifth Amendment and the third Vice-President to occupy the office within a period of about one year.

Rockefeller, generally known as "Rocky," was born in Bar Harbor, Maine, on July 8, 1908, into a family of tremendous wealth. His grandfather, the first billionaire in United States history, had made his fortune in the oil industry. From his earliest years, Rockefeller, the third of six children, had dreamed of being President of the United States. He attended Lincoln School in New York City and then Dartmouth College where he studied economics. Following his graduation in 1930, he married Mary Todhunter Clark and, after their divorce, married Margaretta Fitler Murphy (known to her friends as "Happy").

In 1958, Rockefeller successfully sought his first elective office as Governor of New York. He was reelected Governor of New York three times, occupying that office longer than any other governor in New York history. Rocky unsuccessfully sought his party's nomination for President in 1964 and 1968. At the time of his nomination to be Vice-President, he was widely regarded as perhaps the most qualified member of the Republican Party to serve in our second office. Rockefeller died of a heart attack on January 26, 1979, and his ashes were buried at his family estate in Pocantico Hills, New York.

Walter F. Mondale

WALTER F. MONDALE, forty-second Vice-President of the United States, was born on January 5, 1928 in Ceylon, Minnesota. His father was a farmer and later a minister. Mondale attended school in Minnesota and helped finance his own education. In high school, he played basketball and football and ran track. He then attended Macalester College in St. Paul but transferred to the University of Minnesota when his father died. He graduated in 1951. After two years in the army during the Korean War, he attended the University of Minnesota Law School, graduated in 1956, and practiced law for several years. He married Joan Adams in 1955. They have three children.

Active in politics since his high school days, Mondale was appointed Attorney General of Minnesota in 1960 and elected to that office later that year. In 1964 he was appointed to the United States Senate to fill the seat vacated by Vice-President Hubert Humphrey. He was elected to the Senate in his own right in 1966 and 1972. He distinguished himself during his Senate career as an effective spokesman for minority and consumer interests. On November 2, 1976 he and Democratic presidential candidate Jimmy Carter defeated President Gerald R. Ford and Republican vice-presidential candidate Robert Dole.

Mondale was the first Vice-President to have an office in the White House. In the 1980 election, President Carter and he were defeated. Since then, Mondale has combined lecturing with a law practice.

91

George Bush

GEORGE BUSH was born on June 12, 1924, in Milton, Massachusetts. His parents, Dorothy and Prescott Bush, moved to Connecticut when he was a child. Bush's father served as a United States senator from Connecticut.

Bush attended the Greenwich Country Day School and then Phillips Academy in Massachusetts. In 1942 he enlisted in the Navy and became one of the youngest commissioned pilots. He also received a number of medals for his courage and heroism.

In 1945 Bush married Barbara Pierce and they became the parents of six children, one of whom died. Bush also entered Yale in 1945 where he excelled in both his studies and baseball. Upon his graduation, with a degree in economics, he moved to Texas. He worked in business for a while and started several oil-related companies. He was an unsuccessful candidate for the Senate in 1964 and 1970 and was elected to the House of Representatives in 1966, serving two terms. He then served as the United States delegate to the United Nations, national chairman of the Republican Party, special envoy to Peking, and director of the Central Intelligence Agency.

Bush was considered as a vice-presidential possibility by Presidents Nixon and Ford and was chosen to be President Reagan's running mate in 1980. On January 20, 1981, he became the forty-third Vice-President of the United States.

Index